I AM DEEPLY GRATEFUL . . .

Lawrence Welk talks about himself and his family, about his childhood back on the farm in North Dakota, about the shy beginnings and early hopes of his career, about the wonderful people he has known and worked with, the exciting new talents he has discovered, and, finally, his inspiring belief in the traditional virtues of hard work, commitment, and personal involvement.

I TRIED TO FIND SOME WAY TO EXPRESS MY APPRECIATION

MY AMERICA, YOUR AMERICA

LAWRENCE WELK

with

Bernice McGeehan

A KANGAROO BOOK
PUBLISHED BY POCKET BOOKS NEW YORK

MY AMERICA, YOUR AMERICA

Prentice-Hall edition published 1976

POCKET BOOK edition published November, 1977

This POCKET BOOK edition includes every word contained in
the original, higher-priced edition. It is printed from brand-
new plates made from completely reset, clear, easy-to-read type.
POCKET BOOK editions are published by
POCKET BOOKS,
a Simon & Schuster Division of
GULF & WESTERN CORPORATION
1230 Avenue of the Americas,
New York, N.Y. 10020.
Trademarks registered in the United States
and other countries.

ISBN: 0-671-81410-9.
Library of Congress Catalog Card Number: 76-20456.
This POCKET BOOK edition is published by arrangement with
Prentice-Hall, Inc. Copyright, ©, 1976, by Lawrence Welk.
Pictures (unless otherwise credited) belong to the personal
collection of Lawrence Welk. All rights reserved. This book, or
portions thereof, may not be reproduced by any means with-
out permission of the original publisher: Prentice-Hall, Inc.,
Englewood Cliffs, New Jersey 07632.
Printed in the U.S.A.

FOREWORD

As I WRITE THESE words, our country is approaching its two-hundredth birthday . . . and I am deeply grateful for the privilege of being able to help celebrate it. I, myself, am now in the seventy-second year of a life which just seems to become more and more wonderful as time goes by, and I am filled with deep humility and gratitude for the continuing goodness of God.

I am grateful for something else, too. I know that this wonderful life of mine could never have happened anywhere but here. My parents knew this long before me. Searching for freedom, they came to this country as immigrants, from a land where they, and their parents before them, had been bitterly oppressed—trapped in a life where there was little or no chance to better themselves.

But in this country they found they could go just as far and just as high as their initiative and talents would take them. Nobody told them what kind of work they had to do, or how much they could earn, or where they had to live, or what religion they would have to practice. The only thing their new country asked of them was that they do their very best . . . and to the end of their days my parents remained passionately grateful for this priceless gift of freedom.

I have always felt the same way myself. And as our Bicentennial drew near, I tried to find some way to express my deep appreciation for the privilege of living in this wonderful country.

And it came to me that during the fifty years I have been working in the music business, I have come across certain philosophies, certain truths, which have made my way easier, brightened the path ahead, or given me fresh hope when things looked bleak. During those same fifty years we had created, little by little, in our Musical Family, a sharing and self-development program which had welded us together so tightly, with such love and concern for each other that we had been able to achieve one major professional goal after another. At the same time, we had been able to build personal lives of increasing fulfillment and joy. Somehow, we had stumbled onto a formula to find business success and personal happiness at the same time. We had found a way to get the very best out of ourselves.

I saw this demonstrated over and over again. Older members of the band would begin to develop themselves to such an amazing degree that we all benefited. And the progress of our younger members was equally satisfying. When they first arrived to join our group, they were often a little scared, a little unsure . . . perhaps even a bit confused as to basic moral standards. But working within our family formula for success, they soon began to emerge as self-confident, responsible young adults, the kind who would be a credit to any family, any business, any nation. The kind who could ensure future greatness.

It occurred to me then that one of the best ways I could say "thank you" would be to share this knowledge which had been so helpful to us. What we had been able to do in our Musical Family on a limited scale could be done for our great American Family on a nationwide scale. We could give our country the finest birthday gift of all—dedicated young citizens who could help us become as strong and as free as our founding fathers intended us to be!

So in the pages ahead I will describe how this concept of ours works; how our members (both those in front of the cameras and behind the scenes) have used it to improve their lives; how I, myself, have used it to deal with the pressures and heartbreaks of life; and how I feel, with all my heart, that this method of working freely together can be so very valuable to us all.

I have lived a long time now and received more than my share of honors and accolades. I have known the joys of a warm family life, and that of my wonderful Musical Family, as well as the affectionate regard of thousands of our good friends across the land . . . and I am thankful beyond measure for this outpouring of love. I can only feel that the Good Lord has had His arms around me, when I count the wonderful blessings of my life!

One of the greatest of these, of course, is living in this country. Our nation, with its free-enterprise system, has endured and served us well for two hundred years. In this book, I will try my best to convince you that we should hold on to it, and make it stronger, so it can live for another two hundred. We can best do so by developing within our young Americans the same kind of moral fiber that originally created the best country in the history of the world—My America . . . and yours.

CONTENTS

9

CONTENTS

PART ONE

THE
CHALLENGE

1

MY NEW GOAL

MY MUSICAL FAMILY HAS always had something of a problem with me—I keep coming up with new goals. And I've been that way as far back as I can remember. I've always had a dream, a goal, something to strive for. My first goal was simply to grow big enough so my feet would reach the pedals on our family pump organ. And as soon as Nature obligingly helped me out on that one, I set myself another . . . to have my own accordion. After that, I worked toward getting off the farm and into a musical career, and then toward getting my own little band, and then getting us on radio, and then into the world of the Big Bands, and finally—into television.

I had no idea, when I formed my little four-piece band in Yankton, South Dakota, in 1927, that someday I'd have a Musical Family of more than fifty people, or that we'd be on television for more than a quarter of a century. But looking back, I can see how each one of those goals led quite naturally to the next. (I think life is like that. It has a way of leading you on. The trick

13

is—be ready for it!) And suddenly . . . at the age of seventy-two . . . all my prior goals seemed to merge together and lead me into the most compelling, most powerful goal of all, one that simply took over my life.

In a way, it happened rather slowly. It was during the sixties when I first began to realize we had stumbled onto something very unusual in our Musical Family. We had not only managed to stay on TV successfully year after year, something pretty rare in such an unstable profession, we had also managed to stay together with a closeness and warmth that were . . . to use my favorite expression . . . just plain wonderful. And in the process, we have elevated our own character.

When I talked to other businessmen about this unusual state of affairs, they often confessed how unhappy they were with the lack of cooperation in their own organizations. "Welk," they said, "you are really a lucky guy! Your people are terrific. Yet so many people these days just don't want to work. They don't seem to care any more." That set me to thinking, too. It was certainly true that most of our group worked with tremendous enthusiasm . . . even dedication.

I wondered about it. Were we just plain lucky? Was I such a fortunate fellow I always managed to pick out people of rare talent and character?

I didn't really think so, because we often took youngsters of apparently moderate talents into our own group . . . only to watch them blossom into stardom later on. And many times I had seen some of our people overcome serious personal faults which could have stopped them completely otherwise. That wasn't luck . . . that had to be something more! When I analyzed it over the next few months, I finally realized what it was. We had our own Plan. Our own System. Almost without realizing it, we had worked out our own formula

for success. Through a process of trial and error . . .
through the experiences of a lifetime spent working with
all kinds of people in my band . . . I had discovered
certain basic principles which really worked. They
formed the heart of our Plan, and the more I thought
about it, the more I realized we really did have a
formula which was extremely effective. And yet it was
so simple it could be adapted by anyone who wanted
to give it a fair try.

The thought galvanized me, and I decided to turn
my ideas over to the American public for their consideration. I felt sure that when the average businessman understood the thinking behind it . . . in particular,
how it could transform the lives of young people . . .
he might like to try it out. And that alone was enough
to make me want to spread the word.

But there was something even stronger urging me
on. I felt, deep in my heart, in my very bones, that since
we had found a way to get the best out of ourselves on
an individual basis, we might also be able to help the
nation as a whole.

That thought touched me deeply. I love this country
so much and have, ever since my earliest days on the
farm, and I've always wanted to help this nation that's
been so good to me. Now, for the first time, I felt I had
a real answer to many of the problems facing us—a way
to help us become the whole and happy and dedicated
America we used to be. That made me want to do
everything I could to get our ideas across . . . or at
least give folks a chance to consider them.

At first, I felt like going on TV and telling the whole
world, but I couldn't do that, of course, even though my
Musical Family was certainly a great advertisement for
me. And I didn't have the time to go on a speaking
tour. (Or the talent, either. I knew our Plan could

work wonders . . . but not miracles!) So perhaps a book would be the best answer.

Prentice-Hall had been asking me to do another one, because my first two, *Wunnerful, Wunnerful!* and *Ah-One, Ah-Two!,* had both been quite successful, thanks to our good and loyal fans. I had been saying no, but now I thought it might be the perfect way to express my philosophies. So I called my writer, Bernice. She had worked closely with me on the first two books, and we were still speaking, so I thought she might be willing to work on another. "It's about our Plan," I told her. "I want to tell the folks about it."

When she agreed, I called Prentice-Hall and told them I'd decided to go ahead and do another book for them. "Wonderful!" they said, or words to that effect. "We've been hoping you'd do a book for the Bicentennial year, Mr. Welk. What's the new one going to be about?"

I thought for a moment. "Well," I said, "basically, it's about the development of the human spirit—as seen through the eyes and hearts of the boys and girls in our Musical Family."

I was anxious to get started. I felt a tremendous urgency to share the things I had learned, the accumulation of knowledge garnered over more than seventy years of living. So I cleared myself of every extra appointment for the year ahead, canceled some of my mini-vacations and even—regretfully—crossed out a few tentative golf games. And early in January I sat at my desk in our music room overlooking the lights of Santa Monica . . . and began to write of the things that were deep in my heart.

2

INHERITING NEW DRESSING ROOMS

TWENTY-ONE YEARS AGO, when I first began broadcasting over the ABC television network, I was assigned a small dressing room. Very small. In fact, it was so small it could barely accommodate a desk, a chair, and a telephone. Not only that, it was situated right outside the men's room, so the traffic was always pretty heavy. But I didn't mind. I had spent too many years on the road, changing clothes in everything from a corn field to a broom closet, to care very much about dressing rooms. All I cared about—and cared very much—was to put on the best show possible . . . one that would really please the people.

So I stayed very happily in my tiny little room. Meanwhile, however, ABC signed Frank Sinatra to do a show for them, and—in an effort to show their appreciation for their brand new star—they presented him with a gorgeous new dressing room. Actually, it was a trailer, but it was at least as big as a mobile home and twice as fancy. I used to see it parked right outside Studio E when I arrived to do our weekly show, and I was really impressed. It looked to me as if it would be very plush inside . . . and it was, too, as I found out at the end of one season when Mr. Sinatra suddenly departed the network . . . and I inherited his dressing room.

I really loved that trailer dressing room, too, because it had all the advantages of being outside in the fresh air and sunshine, as well as being fairly close to the stage, and I used it very happily for the next couple of years.

Meanwhile, however, ABC signed another big name, Jerry Lewis, to do a show, and—in an effort to show their appreciation for their brand new star—they built a gorgeous new dressing room for him. Now if Mr. Sinatra's had been grand . . . this one was supergrand! It was built right next to the stage and featured a compact dressing room and bath, something we certainly didn't have on the farm, a small office, a huge reception area furnished with two nine-foot-long brown tweed couches, a big coffee table, a closed-circuit TV, and a vibrating chair. Very nice, too, as I discovered at the end of the season, when Mr. Lewis also departed the network . . . and I inherited *his* dressing room!

There I stayed very happily for the next several years until that black day in 1971 when ABC canceled our show. Dressing room facilities were the furthest thing from my mind at that time, as we all worked hard to secure a place for ourselves in syndication; and it didn't matter to me one bit when ABC reassigned me to a new and very small room. (We had decided to stay on and rent the same facilities at ABC.) My new room was even smaller than the first, but at least it wasn't outside the men's room, so that much was an improvement.

And ABC had put me in the new room only because they had signed the wonderful English actress Miss Julie

Andrews to do a series for them, and—in an effort to show their appreciation for their new star—they had decided to redecorate my old quarters for her. I was actually delighted by this, because I've always had such great admiration for Miss Andrews that if ABC hadn't offered to do so, I might have done it myself. I heard rumors from time to time about how gorgeous her new dressing room was, but I never got to see it because orders had gone out that no one but Miss Andrews was to use it . . . and, in fact, nobody else was even to peek at it. Still, rumors persisted that it was really something . . . and sure enough it was, as I found out at the end of one season when Miss Andrews also departed the network . . . and I inherited *her* dressing room! (That's the first time I've ever inherited a lady's dressing room . . . at least so far.) And I must admit I was awed into silence when I first saw it—pale yellow rug, yellow walls, bright paintings, flowers, lots of mirrors, crystal lights, and even a white telephone. It was so grand I felt like tiptoeing whenever I came in, and I used to think, "Boy, if the folks in Strasburg could only see me now!" I stayed there very happily for the next three years until August 1974 when my Musical Family and I went on tour with my old and good friend Lon Varnell.

When I returned two weeks later, I went to ABC for our regular weekly taping, walked down the hall with the stage manager to my beautiful dressing room, opened the door—and stopped dead! If it had been gorgeous before, it was super-gorgeous now! There was new nylon carpeting on the floor, new twin damask sofas facing each other across a mammoth gold leaf coffee table, a huge chrome-and-glass shelf arrangement against one wall, pots of ceramic azaleas sitting on end tables, a huge white china dog peacefully surveying the scene

19

from one corner, and a dimmer switch on the wall which threw the whole thing into startling brilliance. I stood rooted to the spot, almost overcome with all this magnificence, and my jaw dropped so far it was practically on my chest. Finally I managed to burble, "My, my, my! Oh, this is gorgeous, just gorgeous! My goodness, you really didn't have to go to all this trouble just for me! Honestly, you didn't!"

The stage manager began to look uncomfortable and shuffled back and forth from one foot to the other. Finally, he said awkwardly, "Uh . . . well, to tell you the truth, Mr. Welk, this here's not for you. This here's for Sonny Bono."

It was all too true. ABC had just signed Sonny Bono to do a show for them, and—in an effort to show their appreciation for their new star—they had redecorated my dressing room for him. History was repeating itself, in more ways than one, because exactly six weeks later Mr. Bono also departed the network . . . and once again I inherited a new dressing room!

There I stayed for another season, until a massive reshuffling of studios moved our entire show to Studio D, where I now have plush headquarters in a downstairs dressing room reached by a curving stairway, reminiscent of the kind found on submarines. In fact, my old friend Barney Liddell says the sight of me rising from that spiral staircase to bound out onto the stage, always reminds him of a U-boat captain rising from the deep to issue orders, and he has to restrain an impulse to salute. The new quarters are neither as plush as some we've had, nor as Spartan . . . but they are clean and comfortable, and that's all I've ever asked. As long as our facilities are clean, and our girls have a comfortable and convenient place in which to change that's all that matters. The most important thing—the only important thing—is to do the job well. If we didn't do that, we wouldn't have to worry about dressing rooms or telephones or anything else. We'd be too busy looking for another job! To live a successful life, you must be able to distinguish between which things are important and which things are not. And the best time to begin learning that . . . or anything else . . . is when you're young. Very young.

3

SIX LITTLE GIRLS

STARTING "YOUNG" IS ONE of the theories on which I've based my life. That, and learning your trade through actual experience. So when the Semonski sisters came along in 1974, it gave me an almost perfect chance to try out my theories on the development of young people. I'd actually done it many times before with individual stars, perhaps most notably with the Lennon sisters. But the Semonskis offered an even more perfect test case because they were younger, and had had no professional experience of any kind. In fact, I was the only one who could see any potential in them at all! The rest of my right-hand people were woefully discouraging.

George Cates, my musical director, spent close to an hour trying to talk me out of the whole thing, following me around my dressing room one evening while I was getting ready for the show. "The thing is, Lawrence," he said, as I was shaving, "trying to train six little girls who've had no experience would be a tremendous undertaking . . . an impossible job! They're completely green." "Mmmm," I agreed, running the razor over my

22

chin. "You have a strong point there, my friend." "And with six of them," he went on, "the expenses would be overwhelming!" "Yes, you're no doubt right about that," I said, unplugging my razor and running a comb through my hair. "And not only that," he said, following me into the makeup room where Rudy Horvatich began putting a light coat of pancake on my face, "not only that, but think of the costumes! For six people . . . and a special one for the little one . . . she's only seven-and-a-half years old, you know." "Yes, I know," I told him, mumbling through stiff lips so I wouldn't ruin Rudy's makeup job. "I won't forget." "And another thing, have you thought about taking them on tour? Hah! Why those expenses alone would eat up the budget!" George paused . . . he knew he had struck a nerve with that one. "George," I agreed, "you've really analyzed the situation. That's wisdom—pure wisdom!" He nodded. "And, Lawrence, have you thought about the headaches you'll have hiring youngsters this age? All but one of them under eighteen? Look what you've got there, you've got the social service agencies, and the child labor laws, and all those other restrictions that don't allow young people to work, have you thought about that?" "Yes, indeed," I said with feeling. "I certainly have thought about that!" "And, Lawrence, don't forget"—he jabbed his forefinger into my chest to emphasize his point— "even if you spend a full year training them . . . you have no assurance whatever that they'll make it!" He stopped, sure he had me convinced. "Well," I said, shrugging into my coat and adjusting my tie, "I can certainly see you've given this a lot of thought, George, and I appreciate it. I really do. And you're probably right. It would no doubt be a tremendous job to take them on." Then I went out and hired them.

I really wasn't as flippant as I sounded. I had several

reasons for doing so, even though the thought of contending with all the California state child labor regulations made me think twice. But I truly did have an instinctive feeling that the girls could be developed. And also . . . they offered a challenge! And I wanted to prove once and for all that our Family Training and Sharing System could develop anyone with a reasonable amount of talent plus a genuine desire to succeed. Of the two, it may have been the challenge that spurred me on the most . . . I'v never been able to resist a stiff challenge! Or, maybe it was just the sweetness, the niceness of the girls themselves. Whatever it was, something made me decide to fly in the face of all the odds, and see what I could do for these six little girls.

I had found them originally in Orlando, Florida, just before Christmas, 1974, where I'd gone to play in the Disney World Golf Tournament. On the way back home, I stopped in to see my good friend Walter Windsor who manages the TV station in Orlando which carries our show. When I arrived at the studio to do an interview show for him, he had the whole Semonski family—Rusty, Joe, and their six small daughters—lined up and waiting to sing for me. I was charmed with them, but there was no way I could bring eight people out to the coast on the promise of just one show. And there was no way I could guarantee anything more without conferring with our production staff. So, regretfully, we said goodbye and I flew home. A few days later, their father called long distance to tell me they'd decided to drive to California for their Christmas vacation. "And if you want to use the girls on the show while we're there," he said, "we'd be delighted." Well, that did it! When the girls arrived, we put them on our Christmas show.

But my staff was notably unenthusiastic after their

first appearance, and the girls more than confirmed my first impression: They were nice girls, sweet girls, but completely unprofessional, lacking that certain little extra that marks the difference between seasoned performers and rank amateurs. I, myself, felt the girls could be developed. But my staff, even though they liked the youngsters very much on a personal level, had misgivings.

We finally decided to let them sing on the New Year's show which we taped the following day, but watching them perform, I realized anew how much training they would require, and what a great challenge they were. I was really in a quandary. On one hand, I wanted to give them a chance. On the other, I knew it would be an almost insurmountable job. But somehow, looking at these six—well, eight really, because the parents were so hopeful, too—looking at those eight eager faces, I just didn't have the heart to turn them down. I finally decided to have the whole family move into our mobile homes resort at Escondido for a while. My thought was that the two oldest girls, Diane and Donna, could work as cashier and hostess in our restaurant there and sing occasionally for the patrons . . . a happy birthday song or an anniversary salute. That would give them a foot in the door, plus a chance to earn a little money on their own . . . something I feel so strongly that young people today need for their development. The rest of the girls could go to the local schools, and all of them could study music and harmony. And if they improved enough, we could use them on the show from time to time.

I'd used this same system before, notably with Anacani, Tom Netherton, and Ava Barber, and it had worked beautifully with all three. So I decided to try it with the Semonskis. Early in January the entire Semonski family drove to Escondido and moved into our guest house at the top of the hill . . . and our great experiment began.

For the next five months I drove to Escondido almost every week to visit the girls, encourage them, coach them, motivate them. I'd drive up the hill to our mobile home where the whole family was waiting for me, and then we'd all sit down on the living room floor, with little Michelle cuddled on my lap, and the girls would sing their latest song for me. Those weekly coaching sessions helped a good deal. But perhaps the fact that I cared enough to make a two-hundred-mile round trip every week or so helped a little, too. It made the girls realize that we truly cared about them and their welfare, and they responded with even more determination to succeed.

We try to do something a little extra like that with all our new people. When Anacani first became our singing hostess at Escondido, we arranged for her and her mother to live right in one of our mobile homes on the grounds, to make it a little easier for her. And when they came to Los Angeles in those early weeks to do the show, they stayed in the apartment our corporation keeps for visiting business associates. When Ava Barber and her husband, Roger Sullivan, first came out, they stayed in that apartment also, until they found a place of their own. And when Tom Netherton first came to town he didn't know a soul, so I more or less took him under my wing for the first couple of weeks.

One night I took him along with us to the Bel Air Club for dinner. He was dazzled with the surroundings, the spectacular view of Los Angeles through the huge picture windows, and all the famous names sitting around the dining room. "Oh, look, there's Fred Mac-Murray!" he said, awed, "and June Haver . . . and Carol Lawrence . . . and Robert Goulet! Oh, I can't believe this, it's like a dream!" "Tom," I said, "it's no dream. And you'll be there yourself some day."

I always try to spend time with our newcomers to let them know I believe in them completely, that we picked them out because we like them and want to do the best we can for them. We truly care about them. And when they understand the truth of this . . . they begin to care, too. Its the first step in establishing the unusual bond between us, the warmth, the thing that makes us a "family." And so, as I do with all our new trainees, I went out of my way . . . about two hundred miles! . . . to do something a little extra for the Semonskis.

Of course, it wasn't just the girls that kept me coming back to Escondido every week. It was Escondido itself! It's such a beautiful place, I really love it—like living in the middle of a lush and beautiful park. We have more than two hundred mobile homes climbing up the side of the mountain, with a small but tricky eighteen-hole golf course winding through the foothills. It is so lovely we've filmed several of our television shows there. Sometimes when I stand on the big slatted wooden front porch of our house, which juts out over the cliff, and gaze down the boulder-strewn hillside to the golf course and swimming pools below, and the Escondido mountains fading into the distance all around us, I wonder how I ever got from the Strasburg prairies to all this! In some ways, I guess I'm still a small boy. I've never really grown up. Life is still a wonderful adventure to me.

Every time I go to Escondido, I have a wonderful chance to play all the golf I want to. I get out on the course very early every morning and play with our golf pro, Don Donahue, who does such a fabulous job of keeping the greens in top condition . . . and also gives me some very good golf pointers. Later, I go to the restaurant for a snack or some dinner, and I must say our dedicated chef, Bill Balnaves, makes it pretty hard for me to stick to my diet. As a rule, I am more or less inundated with requests for autographs or pictures during my meals, but I never mind it. In fact, I enjoy it and often lug my accordion along in hopes the folks will ask me to play. Our fans are the ones who make our life possible, and I'll never, never turn my back on them—even when my hamburger is halfway up to my mouth! Paul Ryan, our manager, said to me one night, "Lawrence, I feel so sorry for you. You never got to finish a single meal today!" "That's okay," I told him. "I can always eat. I can't always meet our fans in person."

I had found Escondido almost by accident, about twelve years before. My business advisors, Ted Lennon and Bert Carter, had lined up some orchards in the Southern California area which they thought might be a good investment for us. So one day the three of us drove down to take a look at them, talking nonstop all the way. The closer we got to San Diego, the more lush and lovely the countryside became, and soon we began passing beautiful avocado orchards, orange and lemon groves, rich farmland dotted with ripening melons, and huge strawberry fields—it all looked very interesting indeed. But about thirty-five miles north of San Diego, on Highway 395, we passed a new mobile homes resort set into the side of a curving mountain with a little nine-hole golf course spread out in front of it—that looked even more interesting! (My mind is never very far away from golf.) "Let's go back and take a look at that," I suggested, and Ted wheeled around and headed back up 395 for a closer look. When we drove in we found a small restaurant there—more of a lunch counter, really—and decided to have some lunch. The manager joined us and we chatted for a while and finally I asked to speak to the owner, Harold Squires. "Well, he's not here today," said the manager, "but Mrs. Squires is. Would you like to talk to her?"

"I certainly would," I said, and we all waited while he called her on the phone. "Say, Mrs. Squires," we heard him say, "I've got Lawrence Welk here in the lunchroom and he wants to talk to you. Can you come over right away?"

We waited and made idle conversation and waited some more . . . but still no Mrs. Squires . . . and finally I began looking at my wristwatch. "Can't understand what's keeping her," said the manager worriedly. "I better call her again." When she answered, he hissed, "Listen, Mrs. Squires, can't you hurry up? Lawrence Welk is here waiting for you!"

"Oh, sure he is," said Mrs. Squires. "Listen . . . it just so happens I know today is April 1st!"

"I'm not fooling. He really is here," insisted the manager. "Come see for yourself!" A few minutes later the door suddenly flew open and in walked a lady wearing bedroom slippers, a bathrobe, a "show-me" look on her face and curlers in her hair. When she saw us, her jaw dropped and she turned and fled, shrieking, "Oh, no, it really is him; oh, I could *kill* you!"

Presently she returned, smiling, looking very nice indeed . . . a truly lovely lady . . . and we had a pleasant conversation. The upshot was that we met with Mr. Squires a little later, and after a few more meetings . . . Escondido was ours! And I've never regretted it. It was a big investment for a musician like me to make, and I was pretty nervous at the time, but it turned out very well . . . and during those spring months in 1975, it became increasingly important in our lives.

4

WORK!

I BEGAN TO WORK out something of a routine for myself
in the next few weeks, as I tried to coordinate all my
goals—oversee the show, train our kids, produce a new
series of recordings, and . . . write my book. I'd planned
to write a short, concise outline of our Training and
Sharing System as an opening chapter, but I was finding
it quite difficult. "Don't worry," Bernice would say,
"we'll get it. Just tell me again how the System works."
So I'd tell her, she'd write a rough chapter, I'd read
it . . . and then we'd work some more!

Meanwhile, I worked out a new schedule for myself.
Up at dawn (more or less; I don't use an alarm clock,
I just seem to wake up naturally). Then into the shower, a few laps in the swimming pool, a simple breakfast
with Fern, maybe a short session in the back yard hitting
golf balls into the netted screen I have rigged up
there, and then down to my office. I was almost always
the first one there. My secretary, Lois Lamont, once
groaned, "Lawrence, I give up! No matter how early

I get here, you're always here first!" I'd check over the day's schedule, greet the early arrivals, and then . . . as I began working seriously on the book . . . telephone Bernice with some new thoughts. At seven-thirty in the morning she wasn't always too thrilled to hear from me, but as I pointed out, my mind always functions better at that time of day. Then I'd get to work mapping out training ideas for the Semonskis, or the other kids . . . making lists of songs I thought they could handle that I could check later with George Cates or our wonderful arranger Bob Ballard. I had so many projects going for myself I almost backtracked and met myself coming.

One day, trying to be super-efficient, I asked my son, Larry, to deliver a stack of records to the Wilshire Country Club while I was playing golf there with Don Fedderson. I figured I could go straight home from the club and get started listening to the records right after dinner. It was a great plan and everyone did his part to perfection . . . except me. I was in such a hurry to get home I forgot the records! Fern and I are really home-bodies and I don't like to keep her waiting for dinner, so I always try to get there before five or six at the latest. And here I was, stuck in the middle of the free-way before I remembered them; so in order not to keep her waiting, I decided to go on home and drive back to the club and pick them up after dinner.

Meanwhile, however . . . back at the club . . . Don had noticed the records and taken them home with him! Well, Don lives in Encino, I live in Santa Monica, and the club is in Hollywood. By the time I got back home again, to find that Don had had the records delivered to me . . . I had driven about fifty miles, and I was too tired to listen to them, anyway! I decided I'd better take a refresher course in my own System and get a little more organized. Meanwhile, I fell into bed and got a good night's sleep.

As I worked with the Semonskis, I kept notes on their progress to include in the book. I wanted to see how well our theories could develop young people, even youngsters as raw and untrained as these little girls. I went very slowly with the girls to start with, partly because that's a basic axiom of mine . . . "build slowly but thoroughly" . . . and partly because they were just so young and unprofessional we couldn't have gone fast even if we wanted to. What little training they'd had hadn't been too helpful. Somewhere along the line they'd been taught to move around while singing, in some sort of choreography. But, as I explained to them, it's far more effective on television if the camera can move in very closely, so close you can see the expression in the performer's eyes. And trying to focus on six little girls all jiggling at the same time was clearly an impossibility. So . . . "Stand still!" became almost a password. Every time the girls would forget and start bouncing, I'd put on my sternest expression and say, "Girls . . . stand still!" And the girls would collapse onto each other's shoulders, giggling and squirming in embarrassment— but they'd stand still. At least for a little while. Habits are difficult to overcome.

And, as we worked together, I also began to amass notes on the myriad requirements involved in working with youngsters. There were so many union and labor restrictions and such mountains of red tape that I literally ached to get them changed or set aside so we could work with a little freer hand. In fact, along with spreading the word about our Family Training and Sharing System, that became another new goal in life. But when

I told Fern about it, she sighed deeply. "You know, Lawrence," she said, shaking her head, "I think I'm going to give up on you!" I laughed. I knew what she meant because I had more or less promised her years before that I'd retire when I was sixty-five. And here I was at seventy-two, still going strong, and setting new goals for myself! In fact, they practically took over my life. I thought about them all the time. I woke up in the morning with thoughts running through my head, and as I churned up and down the pool, taking my morning swim, my mind would also be churning with new thoughts, new ideas. I kept a notebook with me to jot down my ideas. And I read books and took copious notes.

What I wanted to do was not only get the System that had worked so well for our Musical Family across to the public, but also get them interested in making some changes that would give the whole nation a little more freedom. It was certainly an ambitious project on my part, and maybe if I weren't so determined, so persistent . . . well, all right, just plain stubborn! . . . I would have given up even before I got started. But I couldn't. Because what I was proposing wasn't just some wild-eyed visionary dream. It was a Plan based on ideas which had been tested and refined in our own Musical Family, a formula which had been forged in the crucible of hard life-molding experience. Nothing in life is foolproof, of course. But our Plan had been tried and proven again and again for more than half a century. I felt it was worth telling the public about. In fact, I felt it would be wrong not to tell them.

That was really what had impelled me so strongly into working with the Semonskis, although I must confess I was pretty shaken when I first started training them. I found myself in deep trouble right off the bat, because the girls just didn't know how to work! They thought they did. In fact, they looked absolutely baffled when I said, almost in desperation, one day, "Girls, you simply must buckle down and get to work! You've got to learn how to work!"

It really wasn't their fault. Like most other young people today, they'd simply never been given a chance to work, a chance to learn. I don't know what we're trying to prove in this country, but we seem to be going out of our way to prevent young people from learning how to work . . . or to work, period! And yet work—plain hard unadulterated work—is the very essence of life. Everything else depends on it.

W-O-R-K!

"Look," I said to the girls, "look at Bobby and Cissy. Now *that's* what I mean by work!" And I told them about the time at the Palladium Ballroom in Hollywood when I had seen a stunning example of work translated into high art. We had a huge crowd that particular night, jampacking the place, every table set up and crowded together, barely enough room on the dance floor for people to move. The band was in top form, the audience highly responsive, and I thought, rather smugly, that we were doing a pretty good job of entertaining. But when Bobby and Cissy whirled out onstage to the strains of "In the Mood," it was as if we'd been standing still doing nothing for the previous hour! Watching their breathtaking performance, the skill and beauty with which the two of them spun through their routine . . . the audience exploded with enthusiasm! It was as if a current of lightning had suddenly struck and lighted everything up . . . the starlights hanging from the chandeliers overhead, the spotlights crisscrossing the audience and pinpointing the dancers onstage, the smiles lighting everyone's faces, the glow in Bobby's and Cissy's eyes, the glow in my own heart. Standing at one side of the platform, watching their exhilarating performance, I was just one big goosebump from head to foot! But even in the middle of that tremendous excitement, and the music and lights and rhythm, and the insistent, over-whelming applause, I was aware (hardheaded German that I am) that all that joy had been brought about by sheer hard, persistent, dogged, untiring day-after-day work! How many times had I seen those two young perfectionists rehearsing until Bobby, dripping with per-spiration, a towel flung around his neck, would race off to his dressing room to shower and change. Cissy, also, placed such demands of perfection on herself that she was never quite satisfied. One time she and Bobby had done a Filipino pole dance, the Tinickling, on the show . . . an intricate routine which involved hopping in between two long bamboo poles which two other people clap together, and somehow Cissy missed a step and got her ankle caught. She burst into tears of frustration the moment the show went off the air. "Oh, Lawrence, please let me do it again!" she begged. "Please! I know I can do it; I know I can do it right!" I'd thought the little misstep was kind of charming and I wanted to keep it in, but she was so upset that we taped the num-ber again.

"And that's what I mean by work!" I told the Se-monski girls. "You have to throw your whole heart and soul into it, and keep at it till you get it right."

Of course, it was no real wonder the girls hadn't learned how to work like that. Our whole culture today seems to assume that work is something to be avoided, something to get out of the way so we can get on with the real business of living. And yet there is a joy, a spontaneity, a release, in the act of work itself which can do more for you than anything else I can think of. Philosophers down through the ages from Socrates to Bishop Sheen have spoken of the cleansing powers of work, of the beauty, the fulfillment of it . . . and I agree. I can't speak in the eloquent terms they do, because I'm a plain man speaking plainly. But I agree completely with Thomas Carlyle who said, "Blessed is he who has found his work." There is a joy, a nobleness, almost a sacredness in work . . . any kind of work. It can strengthen your inner resolve, give you a sense of accomplishment that truly enriches your life, and bring you peace of mind. It can even give you a good night's sleep!

5

TAHOE '75!

IN JUNE WE WENT to Harrah's in Tahoe for our regular three-week appearance. It always seems just like a vacation to us because, after the first couple of days, we're free from the moment our last show ends at one-thirty in the morning, until the next show at eight-fifteen that night. And those long, lovely lazy days in the fresh air and sunshine of Tahoe are always so wonderful. But so is Harrah's itself. In fact, it's always kind of heartbreaking for me to have to leave, because the theater equipment there is so superb. I always feel we have a better chance of really entertaining the folks, because Harrah's has two small side stages in addition to the center stage, and that helps us dovetail appearances far more smoothly. We have something of a problem in that respect. Most shows consist of a star and, perhaps, a small supporting cast. But we have more than fifty "stars," and trying to get them all on and off the stage in their separate appearances in less than an hour-and-a-half is a very complicated job. But Jim Hobson and Jack Imel, our producers, always manage to do it, and this time they had things so well prepared I even had time for a little snooze before our opening-night curtain. The show itself went without a hitch. I was very, very proud of my kids.

I just loved the way it opened—all the girls stepped through a white lattice-work portal while the band played "The Most Beautiful Girl in the World." I introduced them one by one, and I couldn't help thinking how appropriate that music was. They really did look beautiful! Each girl wore a red chiffon gown with a feather boa to match, and a crown of sparkling rhinestones in her hair. Sandi led off the parade as "our young lady from Brigham Young University in Provo, Utah"; then came our Ralna from Lubbock, Texas; then Tanya, "my Italian daughter-in-law"; Cissy from Albuquerque, New Mexico; Anacani from Escondido; Ava Barber from Knoxville, Tennessee; Gail Farrell from Durant, Oklahoma; and finally, little Mary Lou Metzger from Philadelphia, Pennsylvania. Each of the girls waltzed off with a partner after I escorted her to center stage, but by the time we got to Mary Lou, we had run out of partners! So I claimed that happy privilege for myself. I was so very proud of our lovely ladies. As I said in my opening speech to the audience, "When people ask me who picks out the pretty girls for our show, I always say, 'What a silly question! I do! That's my pleasant job.'"

Ralna and Guy, to no one's surprise, stopped the show every night with their version of "Can't Help Falling in Love." Joe Rizzo had written a powerful arrangement which started out quietly and then built to such a breathtaking climax the audience always burst into thunderous applause and almost refused to let them get off the stage. And Ralna and Guy always looked so nice standing together hand-in-hand, Ralna in a black chiffon gown embroidered with brilliants, and Guy in a pearl-gray tuxedo trimmed in braid. They were a real high spot. But there were others. Arthur Duncan invariably just wowed the folks with his fast footwork and comedy monologue, and Johnny Zell did the same thing with his trumpet solo. Tom got sighs of approval from the audience, especially the ladies, just by walking onstage. But I think maybe our finale was the most impressive number in the whole show.

I'm sentimental, I guess, and I always will be . . . I hope . . . and that finale always set my blood boiling and made me feel as if I were the luckiest man in the world. Our closing number had the whole band, dressed in red, white, and blue costumes with plumed hats to match, marching right through the audience and then up on the stage. I brought up the rear, banging away on a big bass drum. I always had a little trouble getting harnessed into that drum because, just before the finale Joe Feeney and I would be out in the audience serenading some of the ladies with an Irish song. (We did that, incidentally, so the rest of the kids would have time to change costumes and get ready for the finale.) Then, as Joe took his bow, I'd turn to the audience and say, "Folks, we wouldn't think of letting our Anniversary Show go by without a salute to America and the Bicentennial! So now . . . in music . . . we'd like to express our feelings about this wonderful country we all love so much." As I said the last line, the orchestra, waiting offstage in the kitchen, struck up the opening bars of "Your Land and My Land," something that never failed to send shivers up and down my spine. It also sent me into a mad dash into the kitchen where one of the crew was waiting with my drum, ready to pull the straps over my shoulders and buckle me in tight. Then I fell into position at the end of the line, just in time to join the band as it marched through the red velvet drapes and into the main room itself. It was like an obstacle course every night, then, because everyone would reach out and try to shake hands with me or slap me on the back or pull me over to say something nice as I marched by. "I'm sorry," I'd say, panting a little as I tried to keep up with the band, "but I just can't talk right now!" There were a few nights when the band really lost me and I had to race to catch up, but I never minded. In fact, I loved it. And when I finally did get up onstage and stood there in the middle of our Musical Family, with all the girls wearing white organza dresses, the fellows in snow-white tuxedos, the band in red, white, and blue, a giant American flag behind us, and that warm and responsive audience cheering in front of us . . . well, all I can say is, I meant every word of my closing speech in which I thanked God for this wonderful country and the wonderful people in it.

The band played better than I'd ever heard them, so good we decided to make a recording of the show when we got back to Los Angeles. That record marked our twenty-fifth anniversary in television, and when I heard the first test pressing, I thought it was the best thing we'd ever done. I took the record home and gave it to Fern. "Here," I said, almost ruefully, "here's a present for you, Fern. And you know something? It's kind of sad. It took me seventy-two years before I did my best work."

I was kidding, sort of, but it was quite true that all the taste and judgment and expertise I had acquired over half a century had gone into that recording, as well as the combined experience of our musical director, George Cates, and Bob Ballard and the other arrangers. But it was really the musicians themselves who made that record so outstanding, because playing two performances a night every night for three weeks had given them a total of forty-two "rehearsals" . . . and it showed! They played as close to perfection as I've ever heard them. I've always felt that preparation is half the battle in any endeavor, and all my people know I'd rather have them do one song superbly, than a dozen just so-so. True quality, real excellence, perfection in anything takes time . . . and infinite patience. And that was something else I pointed out to our people constantly!

When we met for the first recording session at the Annex studios in Hollywood, with our long-time sound engineer, Thorney Nogar, it looked as though we were going on a picnic—all the fellows were wearing very casual sports clothes, and the girls, whatever girls wear these days. I just never know about our girls! Onstage, they always look so lovely in long, flowing dresses or colorful costumes, but offstage they could be wearing anything from a granny gown to a pair of jeans. I'm used to it, but I must say my jaw dropped a little when Gail Farrell walked in wearing overalls. "Are those overalls?" I asked incredulously. "Sure," she replied blithely, "they're the latest thing." I couldn't believe it . . . here I'd spent twenty years trying to get off the farm so I wouldn't have to wear them, and now they were high style! Norma, as usual, was looking immaculate in a white cotton-and-lace pants suit. Tanya was wearing a full skirt, a scarf around her neck, and a rose in her hair, and the other girls were wearing whatever suited them and was comfortable. When we're recording, we want room to breathe!

And when we're recording, we arrange the band in a somewhat different manner from the way you see us on television. The strings and reeds are at one side of the room, the brass section at the other, and the rhythm section across the back with George standing in the middle and Myron right next to him, perched on a stool. Ranged around the room are "baffle boards"—padded folding screens used to enhance the sound. The singers stand in the crook of one such screen where they can see George and me, too, standing in the control booth overlooking the whole scene.

The recording went off smoothly. We'd rehearse a number, record it, play it back, and . . . almost always . . . go right on to the next one. That was partly because we'd had such a good chance to prepare ourselves in Tahoe, and partly because we've worked together for so long we've been able to mesh our style and work as a team.

Building an orchestra is a delicate, tedious, time-consuming, painstaking, experimental, frustrating, maddening . . . and wonderful! . . . experience, and I just love it. It isn't enough just to have top-flight musicians, great arrangements, and a good leader—although that helps. What you need is a long-term association so you know the other person's style, and he knows yours, and the leader knows everybody's, and is able to fuse the whole thing together into the best possible blend. It's a great big plus, also, if the musicians respect each other and even better if they like each other, too. In our band we do! That's our secret ingredient, the thing we have going for us.

Years ago, I had problems when two of my fine musicians decided not to like each other. They stopped speaking, and when they had to sit side by side, they'd angle their chairs so one was pointing east and the other one west! I was at my wit's end trying to find some way to get these two grown men to stop acting so childishly, but I finally had to give up because they wouldn't give in. Their bad temper was affecting the morale of the entire band. Fortunately, we don't have anything like that today. On the contrary, our boys respect and like each other so much they often get together and rehearse on their own, partly because they know it will improve the band, and partly, I suspect, because they love it.

Often during that run at Tahoe, I'd arrive backstage about an hour and a half before show time, and I'd hear the sounds of a soaring trumpet coming from one dressing room, a clarinet from another, or a dazzling accordion run (Myron, of course) from a third. It filled me with pride and gratitude. How fortunate to have men so anxious to improve, so willing to work on themselves! They had found the secret of perfection.

But the little Semonskis had not yet found it. I'd brought them along to Tahoe because I thought it would help them. And they did learn more about stage presence and deportment during those three weeks in front of a large and very responsive audience than they had in the six months previously. Twice during those months, they had come up to Los Angeles from Escondido to appear on the show—once on St. Patrick's Day and again at Easter. This time, we'd had a better chance to prepare for them. Our wonderful Rose Weiss had designed pale pink organdy dresses with flower-banding on the skirts, and the girls looked very sweet as they stood together and sang "Easter Parade." Nevertheless, they were still a long, long way from singing as well as I felt they could, and I began to wonder if maybe this time I had bitten off more than I could chew! I worried about it for several weeks and finally decided to take them to Tahoe with us. I felt that letting them spend three weeks performing with the whole Musical Family every night would give us all a pretty good indication of whether or not they could ever make it.

In some ways I was very encouraged, because the

audience seemed to like them. Each night when the girls walked out on stage, single file, with each succeeding sister a little smaller than the one in front of her, there was always a stir of interest. And when the folks spotted little Michelle at the end of the line, there was a warm "aaaaah!" and a big burst of applause. That was very nice, of course, and the girls just loved it . . . but they were still inclined to treat the whole thing as something of a lark, an adventure, a chance to dress up in pretty costumes and bask in the spotlight. They still hadn't fully grasped the absolute necessity of working on themselves with any kind of sustained and concentrated effort. That was understandable, of course, in view of their extreme youth. On the other hand, I knew they couldn't make any real progress until they did. And I had to find some way to get that message across to them.

6

THE LAST OF THE
BIG BANDS

OFTEN DURING THAT RUN at Tahoe, I'd stand in the
wings, just soaking up the music. It brought back the
days when I had first started listening to "real" band
music, years before, over the radio. Those faint, far-
away sounds had enchanted me, and probably instilled
in me my first determination to become a member of
that magical group myself some day. I not only listened
to the radio every chance I got, I bought every record
I could afford—even back in the days when they came
in the shape of cylinders. In those years, our family
didn't have a phonograph, but that didn't stop me. I'd
buy the records anyway, and then find a reason to visit
the neighbors and play them there!

As a young man I had a passion for accordion music
and I collected every recording I could find of the
virtuosos of the day—Pietro Deiro, Pietro Frosini, An-
thony Galla-Rini, and Tom Gutenberg, who actually
came to Strasburg one day, where I heard him in person.
That did it! From then on, I played their accordion

records by the hour, hoping to improve my own technique.

Later, when I had a band of my own, I bought recordings of all the famous Big Bands and played them by the hour, too, just because I loved them so much. I had a particular fondness for Dixieland music, performers like Red Nichols and His Five Pennies, a group of brilliant musicians who played with such flawless style I was in awe of them. I played all Red's recordings till they wore out. Then I went out and bought some more.

And now here I was, in 1975, some fifty years later, still hopelessly in love with music, standing in the wings of Harrah's theater night after night, listening to the sounds of my own Big Band. And one night I realized, almost with shock, that we were the last of the Big Bands. With very few exceptions, there just weren't many others. And we were certainly the only one playing regularly on television. Most of the others were used just to back up the star, and were hidden away off-camera somewhere. It made me a little sad, a little melancholy, to think that the Big Bands were gone forever. They brought so much joy to so many people! I don't think anyone who heard them during the thirties or forties can ever forget them. And even today, young people collect their records, recognizing instinctively the technique, the vitality, the "sound," the tremendous quality of those great bands.

And they did have quality! I can still hear the smooth strings of Wayne King, "The Waltz King," playing on the Lady Esther Serenade radio program, or the crisp perfection of Hal Kemp's famous brass and clarinet sections. What technique! Duke Ellington was also one of my very great favorites, and in later years, I asked Duke if he would let me use his star sax man, Johnny Hodges, so we could make an album together. I was so impressed with Johnny's great ability that I hired twelve of the best arrangers in the business to do arrangements for him, songs like "Someone to Watch Over Me," "Stardust," and "Blue Velvet." Paul Whiteman, known as the "King of Jazz," was also one of my early favorites, as were Isham Jones, Jan Garber, and Guy Lombardo. I loved them all and frequently gave the boys a night off and took them to hear one of those fine bands whenever we were within driving distance. It sparked us, inspired us, kept us on our toes.

George Thow, our resident writer and production assistant, used to be in our trumpet section, and before that was a star jazz trumpet player with several groups, including both the Dorsey Brothers' bands, and Jack Teagarden among others, and he knew a lot about the whole scene. In fact, George is our final court of authority whenever we have a question about those days. He told me one night that the Big Bands actually grew out of the little ones that sprang up in the twenties . . . the ones like I used to listen to on the radio. And in those very early days those little bands were fiercely competitive. The musicians used to practice by the hour to improve themselves. They didn't worry about money. They just wanted to make themselves and their bands better and better, and George told me it wasn't at all unusual for one of them to take a cut in pay and move to another band if he felt the other one was musically superior. (After George reminded me, I remembered how my own boys were always leaving me in those early Dakota days. At last I knew why!)

But the point he was trying to make . . . and one with which I agreed completely . . . was that those early bands were absolutely dedicated in their drive for perfection. They wanted to be the best, and they worked together constantly to improve their sound, their intonation, their style. In those early years, union rules were not so stringent, so they could rehearse together more freely, and they did. They developed the close rapport and teamwork which is so essential to a good orchestra.

When those little bands got better . . . they got bigger . . . and led directly to the Big Bands we all remember—Glen Miller, Artie Shaw, Benny Goodman, Glen Gray, Kay Kyser, the Dorsey Brothers, Woody Herman. But they all retained that same spirit of competition. All of us were caught up in it. I, myself, played many a Battle of the Bands at the Trianon and Aragon in Chicago, and in Tom Archer's ballrooms in the Midwest. But even away from outright contests like that we all competed with each other. We wanted to be the best —and that brought out the best in us. I'd say the public benefited most of all from the great music that resulted.

That's what I remember most from those years—and miss most. That striving for excellence, that refusal to compromise with second best, that determination to excel. It was exhilarating, it was "American" . . . and it raised the level of music in this country. What a pleasure it was to listen to those different styles!

And whenever one of the Big Bands came to town, it was just like a holiday. The moment they announced they were coming, business picked up all over town. Girls would save up to buy a new dress or get their hair done, boys to take their girls to dinner. Restaurants and hotels all did increased business, and, of course, so did everything connected with the ballrooms. It was a tremendous boost for the economy. And when the Big Band finally did arrive—what excitement! Toward the end of the wonderful era, my boys and I were sometimes the "Big Band" in question, and when we drove into town in our big bus or motorcade, we'd find crowds of excited fans waiting to greet us, and sometimes a parade, and newspaper and radio interviews. And always at night—a jampacked ballroom, almost exploding with enthusiasm, filled with joyful, eager crowds.

There was a niceness, a sense of "class" to those days. When I played at the beautiful Trianon, we had men dressed in tuxedos continually patrolling the ballroom, making sure everyone behaved properly and didn't dance too close! A little tap on the shoulder, and the offending culprits would understand and immediately move apart. No one made scenes or caused trouble.

The crowds always looked so nice . . . the fellows all dressed in their best, neatly groomed; the girls looking so pretty. I don't suppose there's anyone among us who doesn't enjoy looking at pretty girls (you can certainly count me in that group!) and I don't think I've ever seen prettier girls than those in the Big Band years —flushed with enthusiasm, eyes shining, glowing from the music and dancing. I'm sure many of my readers will not only agree with my appraisal, they'll add that they met their wives at one of those dances. Many a lifetime romance got its start there. Those happy laughing crowds are something I can never, ever forget. If the crowds enjoyed the Big Band music . . . and they did . . . then the view from the bandstand was pretty nice, too. And over it all, always and everywhere, was the sound of that wonderful, wonderful music.

So why did it come to an end? What happened to the Big Bands? You can get almost as many reasons for their decline and fall as the number of bands themselves, but I don't go along with most of them. I'll agree that changing musical styles and various union demands . . . including a major strike . . . all played a part in ending the Big Bands. But I'm convinced that what actually brought it about was the attitude of some of the musicians themselves. They stopped playing the kind of music their fans wanted to hear, and when they did, the crowds stopped coming.

Why the musicians did this, I really don't know. It might have been because union restrictions made it more difficult for them to rehearse together as much as they should, and so they lost their teamwork—the thing that holds a band together. Many of them began to play music for themselves, instead of for the people who came to hear them and dance to them. A few people tried valiantly to keep on dancing, but eventually the crowds began to dwindle down more and more and just drift away from the ballrooms. And the days of the Big Bands were over.

To me that is so very sad, and a little frightening, too, because I can see a close correlation between what happened to the Big Bands and what could happen . . . or is happening . . . to our country. As long as the bands competed eagerly, freely, tried to produce the best "product" they could, operated in freedom so that no one was held back . . . then we had superior bands, a thriving business, and happy people. When they abandoned the principles of free enterprise, and failed to protect their freedom; when they lost their desire to excel, and give of their very best . . . they lost everything.

It makes me unhappy to think this happened to our Big Bands. It frightens me to think the same thing could happen to our country.

At the end of our Tahoe run, I was scheduled to fly home to North Dakota for a little vacation, something I do every year. Before I left I called the Semonskis into my dressing room. "Girls," I said, "I'm going home to Strasburg for the next ten days, and I want you to try a little experiment while I'm gone. I think I may have

found a way to help you take on a little more responsibility and learn how to work on your own." They looked
a little surprised, convinced, I suppose, that they already
knew how. "Now, let's just analyze our association," I
went on. "How much time would you say you need for
sleep every night . . . eight . . . ten . . . twelve hours?"
I got six different answers, but they all agreed twelve
was enough for anybody. "And how much for eating . . .
does three hours seem about right?" Again I got nods of
agreement. "Well, that leaves about nine hours for rest
and recreation," I said, "so do you think you could give
one hour of that time to your profession? Could you devote one hour a day to learning new songs and working
on them?" "Oh, sure, we can," they exclaimed enthusiastically. "Sure we can do that, Mr. Welk!" "That's
fine," I said. "Then would you do one more thing?
Would you make out a little schedule and keep track
of the times you rehearse and what song you're working
on? And then write to me in Strasburg and tell me about
it, tell me what you accomplished?" Again I got overwhelming agreement, bright eyes, and happy smiles, and
we all parted with hugs and kisses and mutual assurances
that we'd all work hard toward our goal. "And don't
forget the letter!" I called, as they left. "Just send it to
Strasburg. They know me there."

Early the next morning, at dawn, I left Tahoe. It
happened to be the Fourth of July, and twice during
the day I landed and rode in Independence Day Parades
—once at Dickinson, North Dakota, and again at Me-
dora, where my good friend Harold Schafer has built a
replica of a turn-of-the-century pioneer town. Harold
and his wife, Sheila, had originally discovered Tom
Netherton for us, so Tom came along, too, to make that
celebration particularly festive. And afterward I went
on to Strasburg for a fine family visit with all my broth-

ers and sisters, plus some wonderful games of golf with my good old friend Buster Hogue of nearby Linton.

My vacation was perfect in every respect but one— I didn't hear from the girls. Every day I walked down the main street of town to the post office to see if my letter had arrived. But it never came. It reminded me of the time over fifty years earlier when I had driven in from the farm every day in my horse and buggy to see if my new accordion had arrived. I drove in every day for three months, and in all that time my accordion never arrived. And now—neither did my letter. I was really disappointed.

When I got home, the girls presented me with a tape of a new song they'd learned and that heartened me a little. But it was obvious that they still hadn't learned how to work, still hadn't learned to take responsibility for doing things on their own.

We had a long, long, way to go.

PART TWO

BEHIND
THE SCENES

7

BEHIND THE SCENES

WE HAD A FEW free days in Los Angeles after I got back from Strasburg before we set out on our regular summer tour. I used the time to catch up on my correspondence, play golf, and work on my book. Jim Hobson and George Cates used it to take off on much-needed vacations—Jim to Hawaii, and George to Japan. The other kids made quick trips home, or just relaxed with their families. And once again, before we left town, I talked with the Semonskis. They were not coming with us because they were nowhere near ready for anything as exacting as a road tour. They were well aware that I'd been disappointed that they hadn't written to me, and so they sat listening, a little subdued, a little solemn. And after I finished, Michelle promised earnestly to learn another chord on her ukulele! (I'd brought her a uke from Hawaii some months earlier and promised her a dollar for every chord she learned. She learned five the first week!)

The girls sat silently as I tried once more to motivate them and help them realize how great their future could be if only they would learn to work on themselves. That's something I do with all our kids, all the time . . . motivate them, paint a picture for them, set up a goal to spark them . . . maybe a goal they had never even considered themselves. Sometimes I overdo it just a little, just to raise their sights. When I first met Anacani, for instance, I was so impressed with her I told her she could become our first woman president if she just set her mind to it. And maybe I wasn't too far off the mark when I said that anyway, because Anacani has a first-rate mind, a good common-sense mind. Even though we were miles apart in age and musical backgrounds (she didn't know a single song I knew or vice versa), we struck up an instant rapport, and she learned so quickly and threw herself into her work with such drive that she became an immediate favorite on the show.

When I finished my pep talk to the Semonskis, they promised fervently to keep track of their rehearsal time and take personal responsibility for practicing one full hour every day. Then the older girls took me aside, and after a few giggles, told me they were already working on a big surprise for me . . . "and we'll have it ready for you when you get back." "A new song?" I asked, smiling at their eager faces. "No, no," they said, "not a song. You'll see!"

So I took off, much heartened by their response . . . and even if I had been downhearted, my spirits would have shot straight up the moment we got on the road. They always do. Meeting our wonderful fans in every part of our great nation, performing for them in person, hearing that massive, wonderful reaction from five or ten or twenty thousand people gathered together, listening to the music we love so much to play for them, is most satisfying.

No wonder I don't want to retire! How could I when

there is so much love flowing across the footlights wherever we go? All of us in the band feel that magic, and even though there are times when touring is a little difficult, especially in the past couple of years with oil shortages and travel restrictions, we still love it! Besides, unavoidable delays and setbacks never bother me. I learned a long time ago that God sends us minor crises and crosses to bear as a way of teaching us. And if we can just keep that in mind, it makes everything much easier, and helps us learn something beneficial from our hardships.

But I must say we have very little chance to learn from trouble spots on our tours, because my good friend Lon Varnell handles them . . . and if there is any way humanly possible to do something without a single error, Lon will do it! I never saw such a man! He's the most highly developed human being I've ever met. When it comes to setting up personal-appearance tours, nobody can compare with him. He travels our proposed route not only once but twice or three times before we ever leave Los Angeles, to head off any problems. He makes sure the arenas and forums are the best available, the parking good, and the sound equipment the very finest. He's a master at preparation, so traveling with him is always smooth as silk. And, as I said in my book, *Ah-One, Ah-Two!* I love to travel with Lon anyway, because I enjoy talking with him so much. He's from Nashville, and his Southern drawl makes everything he says sound twice as delightful.

But what he says is always worth remembering . . . drawl or no drawl. One evening a group of us were sitting around at dinner and the conversation took a serious turn. We began discussing the real meaning of life—what success means to different people, what motivates us the most, what the prime goal of life really is. All of us expounded at length, trying to explain just what we meant. But when it was Lon's turn, all he said, very quietly and simply, was, "The real purpose of life is to use the potential God gave us in ways to serve and honor Him best." In just a few words . . . he had said it all.

We had a wonderful time on that tour which took us all through the East, parts of the Midwest, and on up into Toronto and Montreal. I just love to play for Canadian audiences . . . as a rule they are so generous with their applause and appreciation—and so polite! When we went to Vancouver, British Columbia, and walked into the lobby of our hotel, the Century Plaza, a bus load of tourists who had taken the ferry over from Victoria to see our concert happened to arrive at the same time. They all beamed and smiled at me, and I beamed and smiled at them and braced myself for the usual onslaught of hugs and requests for autographs. But nobody asked me! The ladies were so polite they simply stood and smiled, and I practically had to ask them to ask me. And that night, the same kind of good manners nearly ruined my big number on the show. I always dance with the ladies in our audience, either just after the show starts or near the intermission or both, and usually there's a mad rush for the front of the house with a great deal of pushing and shoving and cutting in. But this time, when I announced I'd like to dance with them, there was no mad rush at all . . . in fact, there wasn't a rush of any kind, which put somewhat of a dent in my ego. When the ladies did begin coming down the aisles, they lined up again very politely, each one waiting her turn, and nobody tagged in on me at all. I danced with the first lady so long I began to feel like a prime wallflower, and finally I stage-whispered in desperation, "'Ladies, it's okay to tag in—*please!*"

As the tour progressed, Tom Netherton began helping out in the dance department. One evening, I called him back to the microphone after he finished his number, and he returned, a little surprised, wondering what I had in mind. "Tom," I said, "it just occurred to me that here you are . . . a single boy . . . and you're passing up a wonderful chance to meet the pretty girls here. Girls," I added, "wouldn't you like to dance with Tom?" There was some enthusiastic applause, so Tom, grinning shyly, walked down the steps to the floor of the house while girls of all ages and sizes began flying down the aisle to meet him. "Now remember," I cautioned, as we waited for them to arrive, "just you young girls. None of you 'mamas' and 'grandmamas' . . . that's for me!"

Some of the girls hung back a little, so I urged them on. "Girls," I said, "this is your big chance! Here's a boy who's single, saves his money, and is looking for a girl! So come on—git him!" And down the aisles they came—everybody from dazzle-eyed teenagers to youngsters so tiny Tom had to pick them up in his arms to dance with them. There was even a "mama" hiding hopefully in line that night to the great amusement of the audience, and the whole thing went off so well we included Tom and his dancing in every show after that.

We always have fun on tour with our audiences—it's like a big family party. Even when we sign autographs, we have fun. I particularly recall the night a very pretty blonde asked me to sign her souvenir program. After I did, she eyed my picture on the cover very closely and then called up loudly, "Mr. Welk, if you ever get a divorce . . . let me know!" Everybody laughed and I lost no time in telling the boys about the incident. "Well, boys," I said smugly, "you can't think of me as the 'old man' anymore. That blonde lady asked me to call her if I ever wanted to get a divorce!" There was a slight pause and then Jack Imel said, "Well, don't get excited. Chances are she's an attorney!" My boys just never let me get away with a thing. They watch me pretty closely.

Something else happened on that tour that pleased me mightily. I was signing autographs one night during intermission, as always, when I became aware that the whole front of the stage was crowded with the rest of the cast signing autographs, too. It hadn't always been that way. Time was when Myron and I were nearly the only ones to sign, along with Bobby and Cissy and one or two more. But gradually, as we worked together developing closer and closer rapport with our fans, the others began to learn that one of the greatest pleasures in life is to share yourself . . . and that the more they gave to the audience, the greater the return in terms of their own happiness. Looking at that stage jammed from one side to the other every night, with happy people exchanging smiles and autographs, was one of the friendliest and happiest sights I ever hope to see.

Back home after the tour, refreshed and invigorated by the warm response from our fans, we plunged into preparations for our new television season. That meant a round of preproduction meetings with my producer, Jim Hobson, musical director, George Cates, and the rest of the staff, and I was itching to get started. So, bright and early on a morning in late July, I drove down to our office in the Lawrence Welk Plaza at the corner of Ocean and Wilshire in Santa Monica. I was early, naturally, but even so, there were a couple of other members of our office family there ahead of me. I suppose when I talk about our Musical Family, most folks think I'm referring to the performers on TV. But those who are behind the scenes are just as big a part of it, or even more so.

We always start off our day with a coffee klatsch in the lounge at the rear of our suite of offices. Pauline Anderson, Ted Lennon's cheerful, pleasant secretary, and Virginia Burnham, our controller, are always there early. And then there's brown-eyed Margaret Heron, who came to us right out of high school fifteen years ago; Barbara Curtiss, who's been with us slightly longer; Laurie Rector, Lois' sister, who's been here longest of all (Laurie handles the tickets, and the other two the fan mail . . . and all of them do a wonderful job); Willa Hubert, George Thow's pretty daughter who works in our music publishing department; and our "baby," Robin Smith, who's been with us only a year. Looking at that bright pretty group so early in the morning, laughing together, discussing television shows from the night before, exchanging news of the day, I realize again how lucky I am to have such loyal and wonderful workers. By eight o'clock all the girls are at their desks and Julie Jobe, our wonderful receptionist famous for her bright and happy voice, is taking the first of the day's phone calls. Julie is not only a great receptionist, she's a super-sleuth. I can't tell you how many times I've come into the office and said, "Julie, I heard a song about 7:23 this morning on the car radio and I'd love to know the name of it." Before long, Julie is in my office, handing me a slip of paper with the title in question.

And we have one other "member of the family" too,

from time to time—one of Lois' little doggies, which are generally poodles. I'll never forget her first dog, Chantez, who became one of my real pals. Even before I opened the front door of our suite of offices, Chantez seemed to sense it; and no matter where she was, she'd come flying into my office, skitter across the rug and under the desk, and by the time I arrived, be sitting regally in my chair with her forepaws up, greeting me for all the world as if she were Chairman of the Board! Well, that always just made my day for me because I love dogs, and always have.

My routine is pretty much the same every morning. I fix myself a cup of tea, have a little conversation with the girls (find out what our fans are thinking) and then stick my head in the door to say good morning to Dean Kay, the handsome young head of our music publishing companies. Then I walk down the long inner gallery of our office, lined from floor to ceiling with the pictures and awards that are so meaningful to us, stop for a quick "hello" to Jack Lennon, who assists Ted in our properties division, and finally go into my own big corner office which has a superb view of the Santa Monica coastline. It's a pretty fancy office for a farm boy, I must say . . . fully carpeted, with electric drapes, a big desk, a coffee table, a couple of couches, an ornate light fixture hanging from the ceiling, and . . . a necessity for me . . . a stereo to play records and audition tapes.

It's there my day begins, in conference with either Lois or Ted. Generally, especially lately, it's Ted, because Lois says, "Lawrence, I have all these forms to fill out. Could you take Ted first?" Every time I read another news report about the incredible number of forms the government and unions require these days, I think, "Poor Lois! I hope she makes it!" Anyway, I generally start with Ted, and if I needed any proof that our Training System works, not only in the music field but in any field, Ted would be my prize example. He was a talent scout when he first came to work for us—a standard salaried job with a standard list of duties. But Ted wanted to make something out of himself . . . and he did. He went far beyond the normal confines of his job and did such excellent work I began entrusting him with more and more duties. He'd had no real experience working with big business or property management, but he had a keen mind and a desire to succeed. I kept opening the door a little wider, letting him climb a little higher and higher. He learned on the job just as much as our musical trainees only, instead of notes and time steps, he was dealing in big figures and big deals. And he learned so thoroughly, every step of the way, that I came to have great confidence in his judgment and expertise. When the time came for us to build our Lawrence Welk Plaza in Santa Monica, I turned the whole job over to him. "Ted," I said, "if you need me, I'm as close as the telephone. But don't call me unless you can't solve the problem alone. Do it yourself as much as possible. I'm putting it on your shoulders." Well, he did the entire job . . . and did it superbly.

After it was completed, I invited Parker Sullivan (president of the General Telephone Company which occupies fifteen floors of our building) and his right-hand man, Allan Cooley, to play golf with us. Afterward we sat down to lunch, and I said, "What I want to know from you, Parker, is . . . how did my boy Ted here treat you throughout the development of this project? Did he treat you fairly in every way?" Parker paused for a moment and then said, "Lawrence, we had nothing but problems . . . just one thing after another. But we were able to solve every one of them.

And I want to say nobody could have been more fair or just or tried harder to do the right thing than Ted. It has worked out exceptionally well for all of us."

Well, you can just imagine how that made me feel! Ted, who is the executive vice-president of our corporation, is quite literally my right-hand man, just as Lois is my right arm. And it's of tremendous satisfaction to me to know that both of them built themselves up, right on the job.

Lois' story is much the same. When I was thinking about hiring her in Milwaukee, Wisconsin, I sent her on an errand to my accountant and booking agent. Immediately they both called and cautioned me not to hire her. "That girl doesn't know the first thing about show business," one of them moaned. He was right. Lois was just out of high school and knew absolutely nothing about show business. But she wanted to make a good life for herself and her family, particularly her mother, and she threw herself into learning everything she could about her new job . . . to say nothing of learning to understand my English! She became so dependable, so reliable, so informed about every part of our business that today she runs the entire office. I haven't the faintest idea how she handles all the mail that comes through our office. I just know I trust her completely. Lois surprised all of us, happily, when she and Russ Klein, who has played in our saxophone section since 1957, were married in August of 1975.

When she and Russ were planning to be married, they decided to have a very small wedding with only the members of the family present. Lois invited Fern and me to come also, which pleased me deeply, but I was afraid maybe she was just being polite and really wanted to confine the ceremony to her immediate family . . . so I demurred. But a few days later she asked me again. "Well," I said, "I would love to. But Lois . . . so many people love you so much I just wonder if you wouldn't be on the spot, so to speak, if you don't invite the others, too?" Lois considered this for a moment and then she said whimsically, "But, Lawrence, I didn't work for any of the others for thirty years! We want you to come. Please."

So Fern and I attended her small, lovely wedding in the Lutheran Church of the Master, where her close friend, Dr. S. A. Candow, the pastor of the church, conducted the ceremony. He spoke so nicely of what a fine person Lois is . . . it was such a moving ceremony. I couldn't help thinking that Lois' mother, Mrs. Velora Bielefeldt, must be very proud of her daughter. She'd come a long, long way since that day in Milwaukee when I'd hired her right out of high school. She wanted to make something of her life and she most certainly had. I was very, very proud of her myself that day.

It was a happy ending to a tough year for her, because she'd been stricken with a brain aneurysm about a year and a half earlier, and we had all been so very worried about her. But she came through the surgery in beautiful shape, and three months later she was back at her desk. Of course, it took her a few more months to get completely back to normal, and sometimes in those early weeks the two of us were like a comedy team. One afternoon we were trying to answer several letters, and along about four o'clock neither one of us could think of the name of a man we needed to mention in one of the letters. Lois sat and thought . . . and I sat and thought . . . and finally I said, "Well, we're a great pair Lois! Here you are with brain surgery . . . and me with a mind that stops functioning at four o'clock . . . and neither one of us can think. Let's go home!"

But Lois made a fast, almost incredible recovery after that and is right back running things just as she did before . . . only she now has Russ, one of the nicest men I've ever known in my life, to help her.

Our first production meeting for the season was scheduled for ten o'clock in the morning, and both Jim Hobson and Jack Imel arrived early with notes and plans ready to discuss. Both men are highly organized, as are George Thow, who is such a great help to me, and Curt Ramsey, our arranger and music librarian. If you want to know who sang which song on which show at what time . . . if you want to know anything about any of our shows . . . they not only have the information available, they also knew exactly where to find it! I really admire the way they write everything down, because I'm just the opposite. I keep everything filed in my head. That is, I used to, but at my age I can't always pull it out when I want to, so in the past few years I've gotten in the habit of writing little notes to myself, just to make sure.

At this first meeting, George Thow sat in his usual spot next to my desk, George Cates parked himself next to the piano so he could pound out a few chords, if necessary, and our wonderful arrangers, Bob Ballard, Joe Rizzo, and Curt, settled down with their own notes and briefcases, and for the next two hours we engaged in a hot and heavy discussion of all the options open to us in the new season. "I'd like to see us make one change, gentlemen," I said. "As you know, we've had a most loyal mother-and-father audience for all these years, and they'll be first with us, always. But since we're having more and more young people come over to us all the time, I'd like to include some of the best of the new music for them, too. That way, we'll have something for everyone in the family."

Jim nodded. "Right. I agree with you, Lawrence. I think it will be very well accepted."

We had lots of work on the agenda. I never feel comfortable unless we have about six shows tentatively lined up, and at least two or three completely under way, so we worked hard on plans for the first three telecasts. I'd play a record, toss out an idea for a reaction . . . the others would do the same thing, and everybody put in their two-cents worth . . . discussing, suggesting, urging adoption of some idea or theme they felt very strongly about. I have to laugh when I read occasionally that I'm some kind of iron-handed dictator. I just wish folks could sit in on some of our meetings. Some dictator! All of us jump in with our ideas and suggestions, because we work on the principle of doing what's best for the show. It doesn't matter *who* comes up with ideas. What matters is that we do come up with some.

We worked also on plans for all the kids, discussing which one was ready to try something new, who was making real progress, who needed a helping hand. We were all pleased that Ken Delo had displayed such an unexpected talent for working directly with the audience, singing right to the ladies; we came up with some different song suggestions for him. And, of course, we talked about the Semonskis. We were all united in our feeling that they did "young" songs the best, songs with a youthful flavor in keeping with their own appearance.

Sometimes we get very heated in these discussions, but I love it—that whole intense involvement. It gives me the feeling that we are creating something which will bring happiness to people. Sometimes I feel a wave of incredible joy, real happiness, as we work together. How lucky to be able to play recordings, to choose songs which will be best for the show, to talk about our kids and pick out the number which will suit them best, extend their range of capability just a little more; how marvelous to put together a show with music and ideas and excitement . . . and call it work! If there is one thing I've learned in this long life of mine, it's that the greatest joy in life doesn't come from luxuries, money, vacation trips, or just lying in the sun doing nothing. It comes from work . . . but work at something you love. What joy!

I almost hated to leave for my golf date at noon. It was really hard for me to tear myself away. It always is, when all the parts in the puzzle of what makes a good show are fitting together so nicely. But I had made up my mind years before that one of my prime purposes in life was to develop the people in my band. . . . as well as the band itself. And I knew that the best way to do so was to let them do things on their own, take more responsibility on themselves . . . to learn by doing.

I had no real doubts about whether or not they could do it. I considered Jim Hobson to be the finest producer-director of musical shows in television, and George Cates a master at directing our music. Jack Imel had developed himself so beautifully I was just delighted with him, and our arrangers—Curt Ramsey, Joe Rizzo, and Bob Ballard—were all not only exceptionally talented, but exceptionally stable and reliable. And of course George Thow, so quiet, so full of knowledge, was just so valuable. All my right-hand people were tremendous and I was very proud of them. And almost always they came through with plans which were so good, I felt all I had to do was just show up in time for the broadcast.

But there were other days when they missed the mark, when I realized that . . . good as they were . . . they still needed the old man around, still needed a little more experience, a little more actual knowledge. The greatest favor I could do for them would be to let them learn things on their own. So at noon I gathered my things together and said, "Well, gentlemen, you're on your own! If you need me, you know where to find me." And I went out the door, down the elevator to the garage, and got in my car and started driving out Sunset to the Bel Air Country Club. I had just left my right-hand people alone, so they could learn their job by doing it. I was on my way to do the same thing. Only I had a much tougher assignment—golf!

8

THE SWING AND I

I SOMETIMES WONDER WHY I ever kept on trying to play golf after my disastrous beginnings. I had played the game a few times in my early years as I traveled around the country with the band, but not very often. The first time I was invited to play, back in the thirties in Yankton, I turned down the invitation on the grounds that I didn't have any "golf sticks"! And even after I found out they were called "clubs" and not "sticks," I played very rarely. It wasn't until the sixties, when my good friend and doctor for many years, John Eagan, ordered me to stop working so hard and get some outdoor exercise, that I decided to take up golf as a hobby.

I had no sooner started than I received a very pleasant phone call from the Junior Chamber of Commerce. They were sponsoring the Los Angeles Open Golf Tournament at the Rancho Municipal Golf Course, and they wanted me to participate. "Who, me!" I exclaimed. "You must be kidding! I'm not that good, I can barely play the game!" "Oh, that's all right," they assured me. "You don't have to be good. We just need some star names to attract fans to the tournament. Please do help us, Mr. Welk, we really would appreciate it."

Well, the Chamber of Commerce had been very helpful to me in the past. As a matter of fact, they'd told me our Musical Family (and the Palladium) was one of the three leading tourist attractions in the Los Angeles area. "Walt Disney is first," they said, "then you, and then Forest Lawn!" Well, with that kind of compliment, how could I turn them down? So I finally agreed to play. But I was still very leery about it, and the next evening after work I went out to a driving range on Wilshire Boulevard to practice hitting balls. I also invested twenty-five dollars in a series of six lessons from one of the golf pros. But I didn't seem to absorb his teaching too well, and the next day I called the committee back and tried to beg off. "I'm really terrible," I told them. "Just awful." "Doesn't matter," they said, and once again convinced me they needed me.

Twice more in the next few days I called back, but each time they talked me into going through with it. But I was still pretty nervous and it didn't help my self-confidence any when I picked up the morning paper on the day of the big event and found I was to be teamed with Arnold Palmer, then the undisputed king of golfers. That did it! I was ready to pick up the phone and back out all over again. The thought of demonstrating my terrible technique right next to the great Palmer was almost more than I could bear. But I had given my word to appear, so appear I would.

I drove out to the golf course a couple of hours early to practice hittings balls some more—a mistake, as I discovered later—and stayed there till I heard my name being paged over the loudspeaker. Then I left the safe confines of the practice range and marched reluctantly up to the first tee.

The gallery gave me a nice warm round of applause as I came into view, and that helped—applause always has a comforting effect on me—and I smiled and waved happily back. But then Arnie stepped up to the tee and sent a powerhouse drive straight down the middle of the fairway about two hundred and ninety yards, and my new-found composure suddenly deserted me. My smile froze on my face, my knees started to wobble, and oh, how I wished I were anywhere but there! But there was no way out because the announcer was already introducing me, telling the folks not only what a fine orchestra and television show we had, but also what a great swinger I was! (I don't know exactly what he had in mind, but if he meant golf, he was certainly off the beam.) However, I thanked him, pulled myself together, ordered my knees to stop shaking (which they refused to do), and tottered up to the tee. Then I addressed myself to the ball while the gallery watched with interest to see what this bandleader was going to do. I started taking practice swings again, but I guess I took one too many because one of the spectators, apparently goaded beyond endurance, finally yelled, "For crying out loud, Welk, *hit* it!" And I did. But all the practice had evidently sapped my strength because I barely grazed the top of the ball, and it spurted off weakly to the left about fifty yards—and struck a man standing in the front row of the gallery squarely over his heart. Appalled, I raced over while cries of "Oh! Oh! Is he hurt? Is he conscious? Call a doctor!" rent the air. A policeman was standing beside my "victim," urging him to file a report or give his name or call a doctor or do something, but he waved all such suggestions aside. "No, no, no, I'm fine," he said. "Besides, I'm a fan of Mr. Welk's, I only came up here to meet him anyway, and I wouldn't want to harm him in any way."

Well, I was so relieved I hadn't injured him . . . and so delighted to find he was still a fan of mine even after this disaster . . . that I gave him my card and urged him to meet me for dinner after the match.

Then I went back into the game with renewed energy. I was still embarrassed over the incident, of course, and I had visions of the newspapers the next day chortling over the whole fiasco. "WELK HITS FAN!" "WELK DOES MUCH BETTER WITH A BATON." As a matter of fact, they didn't. Instead, they reported the fact that my second swing was much better than my first, and Arnie and I finished in second place for the day winning a trophy, much to my relief and delight.

Afterward, I looked up my friend and took him to dinner. There my ego took a slight bruising . . . but only about as badly as I'd bruised him, I guess . . . because it turned out that he hadn't come up to the tournament just because he liked me so much after all. He also manufactured golf putters . . . and he wanted to sell me one. Under the circumstances, I did the only decent thing—I bought three!

Now a bad beginning like that might have stopped someone else, but being the kind of man I am, it just made me more determined than ever to lick this game, and I made up my mind to succeed. I bought books, practiced, subscribed to golf magazines, practiced again. And I became absolutely hooked on the game! I just loved it. There was something about being in that fresh open air with good friends, walking over those soft greens, listening to the birds sing, that was pretty close to heaven.

And in spite of the fact that my first tournament was such a disaster, it didn't stop me from entering others. Today I'm invited to play in several of them regularly . . . almost always the Phoenix and Tucson Opens, the Los Angeles Open, the Bob Hope Desert Classic in Palm Springs, the Andy Williams in San Diego, and the Disney World Tournament in Florida. And in 1976 I finally managed to play in Byron Nelson's tournament in Dallas. He'd invited me several times before, but I always had a conflicting engagement. So one evening in 1975, when Byron attended one of our concerts, as he does very often, I said, "Byron, I'm going to make a date with you right now for your tournament next year." And we settled it right then and there.

Well, a few months later, as luck would have it, it developed that my wonderful sponsor and very dear friend, Matty Rosenhaus, was being honored as Man-of-the-Year by the Anti-Defamation League in New York at a big banquet in the Waldorf Astoria, something I wouldn't ordinarily have missed for the world. But when I explained the situation, Matty understood completely, and so finally . . . after several years . . . I got to play in Byron's tournament. I had a lot of fun, too, as I do in most of them. When I played in the first tournament of the season in 1976 . . . the Tucson Open, where my good friend Bill Breck, the Dodge dealer, is always my host . . . I had the good fortune of being teamed with Tom Weiskopf on the opening day. Joe Garagiola was the master of ceremonies and kept the crowd highly entertained. When he introduced me, a lady in the gallery shouted, "Mr. Welk, I used to dance with you back in the Dakotas. Can I dance with you again?" "Sure," I called back. "Come on!" "But what'll we use for music?" she asked, running over. "No problem," I said, and using my golf club for a baton, I waved the crowd into singing "Let Me Call You Sweetheart," while she and I danced around the first tee. I might say I never saw so many photographers spring out of the bushes in all my life as we waltzed together. When we finished, I handed her over to a flustered Tom Weiskopf for an encore . . . and let me say right here that he's not much better at dancing than I am on the golf course! But we all had a lot of fun.

In fact, golf has given me tremendous pleasure, not the least of which was the year I shot three holes in one! All three of these epic achievements took place on our own golf course at Escondido, and I was especially thrilled the third time because my whole Musical Family was with me shooting a television special. They had all assembled along with the cameras and lights, to tape a production number at the swimming pool, situated directly above the eighteenth hole, and as I approached I could see all of them watching me. Well, with my whole family and a large group of fans looking on, I was determined to do my best and show off a little, so I really took my time lining up my shot. There was absolute silence (broken only by Joe Feeney's loud stage whisper, "Hey everybody, duck! The Boss is going to shoot!") before I took a mighty swing. There's a slight rise in the contour of the greens at that point so I couldn't be sure what happened. But such a roar went up I thought maybe I'd hit a hole in one. And sure enough, when I reached the green, I found my ball nestled cozily in the cup! I nearly went straight up with excitement, thrilled to think the whole thing had been filmed. Then I learned the awful truth. "Well, no, Lawrence," said Jim, a little uncomfortably. "The fact is, the cameras were turned the other way the hole time you were shooting." "What!" I exclaimed. You're all fired!" Needless to say, I was just kidding.

I've been very impressed with the quality of the men I meet on the golf course . . . impressed, too, with the caliber of the champions. Almost without exception they are very fine men and women. I'll never forget the day I played my first match with pretty little Laura Baugh who was the winner of the USGA Women's Amateur Golf Championship at the age of fifteen. She played so well I couldn't believe it. "How long have you been playing, Laura?" I asked her. "Oh," she said, "since I was about two." "How could you play at that age?" I queried. "I didn't really play, I guess," she said. "But my dad was a scratch golfer and so were my two brothers, and every time they practiced I went along with a miniature club and started to swing, too. And that's how I learned." Laura may have been younger than average, but most of the great ones started early —Jack Nicklaus, Arnie Palmer, Johnny Miller, and so on. I had the good fortune of playing with Johnny in both the Phoenix and Tucson Opens, and in 1974 I was teamed with him again on the opening day of the Bob Hope Desert Classic. (Again I was lucky enough to be teamed with the reigning champion on the opening day of festivities; and again I was so nervous I hit my first ball into the lake!) But along about the fifth hole I calmed down a little, and when we had to wait for the foursome ahead of us to play through, we sat down to chat. "You've developed yourself to such a high degree of perfection, Johnny," I said. "How do you explain it?"

Johhny didn't answer for a moment, just sat there quietly, his blond hair glinting in the hot bright sunshine. Then he said, "My father was a great help to me. He always encouraged me to excel, and he made me feel that practice was . . . not a duty, but a privilege.

So I practiced constantly . . . all the time." Then he added, almost as an afterthought. "And, of course, I started playing when I was five years old."

With those two statements, Johnny had capsuled what I've long believed to be the secret of success: Constant work and an early start—for golf or anything else.

By now, as I've said, I'm absolutely hooked on the game, and I keep thinking if my Training System works so well in other fields, it ought to work in golf, too, and so I keep trying to "do it myself!" Sometimes it pays off. Not long ago, I played with some of my golfing pals, Eddie Shipstad, Judge O'Connor, and Harry Franklin at the Bel Air Club . . . and I shot a thirty-eight on the front nine! Everybody was very impressed with this feat—especially me. "Well, fellas," I gloated, "what do you think of *that!*" They agreed I'd been pretty lucky. "Lucky!" I cried. "Luck has nothing to do with it. That's skill! You know, fellas . . . I just may give up the music business entirely and go out on the golf tour!" Nobody said anything, which was just as well, because on the next nine the Good Lord took over and brought my ego right down to size. I blew the whole thing.

Ah, well. As I've said, golf is a great teacher. It not only develops your mind, your muscles, your skill, and your suntan. It's also a crash course in humility.

9

MY MUSICAL FAMILY

WHEN I SPOTTED THE Semonskis standing in a group across the stage at the first taping of the new season, I knew immediately what the surprise was they had promised me—they had all lost weight! That is, the older ones had—the little ones hadn't needed to. The older ones hadn't been that much overweight, really, it was just that the camera tends to add a few pounds. Jim had told them that they would really have to keep their weight down to normal if they wanted to photograph well. They looked so slim and pretty as they stood there looking at me hopefully that I couldn't resist teasing them. "Oh, dear," I said in a disappointed voice, "you've all put on a little weight!" Their faces fell and then they realized I was teasing them and we all burst into laughter. I was extremely pleased with them. Like most teen-agers, they loved to eat and it had taken real strength of character to stick to their diets.

But far more importantly, they had stuck to their rehearsal schedule, too! "Sometimes we even practiced two hours a day," said JoAnne, the third eldest girl proudly, as Valerie and Audrey nodded agreement. (At least I think it was JoAnne. At my age, I'm lucky to remember the names of the youngest and oldest!) At any rate, when I heard them at rehearsal, I could readily believe it. It wasn't so much that they were singing better—it was that they had more confidence, that little sparkle that comes from doing something you set out to do. There was still no assurance they'd improve enough to stay with us on a permanent basis. But they seemed to have grasped one of the most vital lessons of all . . . how to assume responsibility for their own behavior . . . and from that point of view we were making real progress. I just beamed at the girls, I was so pleased. For the very first time since they'd been with us, I felt we had taken a major step forward.

Of course, the Semonskis weren't the only examples of how well our Training System could work. All I had to do was look around the band and I'd see at least a dozen others—Gail Farrell, for example. Whenever I saw her carrying a sheaf of new arrangements, I remembered the night I'd found her at the Palladium. Gail had come there that night with her date and somehow or other, before the evening was over, she wound up onstage singing with the band. There she stood . . . slim, small, wearing a white pique dress, flat slippers, and two polka-dot bows in her hair, singing "Downtown" in a cute Oklahoma accent . . . and the audience just loved her. When I talked to her backstage later on and discovered what kind of a girl she was . . . small-town, with a solid religious background, and a great eagerness to succeed . . . I hired her. She'd majored in music at the University of Tulsa, and she began learning everything she could from George Cates and our great arrangers, Bob Ballard, Joe Rizzo and Curt Ramsey. In no time at all, she was bringing in arrangements of her own, good enough for the girls' trio and chorus. She did so well that when the Semonskis came along we assigned them to her, and it was absolutely amazing what she did with them. It might have been because they were all so close in age and understood each other's viewpoints so well. Whatever it was, Gail began to come up with numbers exactly suited to the girls. I think one of the most valuable things we did was to let them work with Gail.

Even George Cates agreed with me on this point, which was news, because he and I frequently disagree over the question of talent. In fact, we disagree so often it always tickles me when I prove a point of my own as in the case of Mary Lou Metzger.

When I first hired Mary Lou, George nearly had a fit. He came storming into my office, saying, "Lawrence, what are you doing hiring this girl! She's not a professional! She can't read music, she can't do this, she can't do that, etc., etc. Now listen, Lawrence, you have a professional orchestra. You can't do this to me!"

I waited until he ran out of breath, and then I said soothingly, "Now, George, she seems to be a very nice girl, and I think she could be of help to us eventually. Why don't we at least give her a chance?"

George just glared at me and stalked out, muttering to himself about the impossibility of trying to direct a show with unprofessional, untrained schoolgirls in the cast.

Two years later, he and I were sitting in my dressing room, sharing a glass of milk and some cookies (my usual before the show snack) when he suddenly said to me, "Lawrence, do you know who the most valuable member of your show is?"

"No," I said, between sips of milk. "Who?" I expected him to say Myron or Henry Cuèsta or one of the other musicians.

"Mary Lou Metzger," he said firmly.

I nearly choked on my milk. "Really?" I managed finally. "Now, why do you say that?"

"Well," he said, ticking off her good points on his fingers, "she's an excellent dancer—next to Cissy, she's the best on the show. She can do all our novelty and specialty numbers. She's a fine little actress. She looks good all the time . . . and her attitude . . . well, her attitude is just wonderful. She's a very valuable person."

"Well, well, well," I said, pleasantly, "isn't that interesting! Say, let me ask you something, George. Do you remember what you said when I first hired her?"

George looked startled . . . and then he looked trapped . . . and then he said, uncertainly, "Uh . . . well, no. Well, yes. Well, anyhow she's certainly an asset today!"

"She certainly is," I said smugly, and I had all I could do to keep from saying, "I told you so!"

In one way, though, Jack Imel is just about my favorite success story. He was certainly the original "bad little boy" when he first joined us. He'd just gotten out of the Navy and perhaps it was a reaction to his years of Navy discipline or something, but he was really a wild boy for a while. He loved to spend his money! If he had a couple of hundred dollars, he'd try to make a down payment on a swimming pool; five hundred . . . an expensive car; a thousand . . . a house. He contracted for so many things that Orville Kelman, our brilliant tax expert and auditor, and our own fine controller, Virginia Burnham, both agreed there was just no way Jack could ever pay for everything on the salary he was making. It finally got to the point where we had to route his pay check through the business manager's office before he ever got it, and I was torn between letting him go or giving him one more lecture and one more chance. Fortunately, I chose the latter, and I'm so glad I did, because once we got Jack's enormous creative energy channeled in the right direction, it was just amazing. He began to come up with so many good ideas for the show that we let him try his hand at assisting Jim and do some of the choreography and staging. As his responsibilities to the program increased, so did his sense of personal responsibility. He developed himself to such a degree that he's now our assistant director and is in charge of everything we do on the road. He does it flawlessly, too. The stage manager at Harrah's told me that Jack's meticulously prepared stage and lighting directions were the best he'd ever seen. "It makes our job so much easier," he told me.

Naturally, that was a great thrill to me, because Jack was really difficult in a lot of ways. I asked him one time what accounted for the change. He grinned that "Jack Imel" grin and said, "Well, Lawrence, you really shook me up when you hired Arthur Duncan. He was such a good dancer I had visions of being out on the street looking for a job. I knew you'd put up with a lot from me . . . and I just decided to shape up, that's all!"

Jack had touched on a key point in our philosophy when he mentioned the word "competition." We do have competition in our group . . . but a very healthy kind, the kind that brings out the best in us, not the worst. We're able to minimize any kind of jealousy or envy because we all know the better the show . . . the better for us. Of course, I don't mean to imply that we're all paragons, without any faults. Over the years we've had our share of stubborn characters, our lazy bones, our problem children. But the percentage who have overcome faults . . . some of them very serious . . . is amazingly high. Some of our people have overcome tremendous odds and emerged all the more wonderful, with an even stronger character. We have so many stories along that line . . . some heartbreaking, some poignant, some so personal I wouldn't feel right about telling them. And then we have some like, well . . . some like Barney Liddell!

Barney has been my personal project for over twenty-five years now, and we're still at it, but I have to admit that, in a way, he's made the most remarkable progress of all. Because he's tried to overcome two very difficult faults—eating and talking! He loves to eat, which makes him too heavy for our cameras, and he loves to talk, and even though he tries to whisper, you can hear him clear across the stage.

Barney and I struggled with his main problem—his weight—for years. Several years ago, in Tahoe, his weight really began to balloon, but when I spoke to him about it he insisted he hadn't gained an ounce. "No, no, Boss!" he said. "I still weigh the same as ever —two hundred and twelve pounds!" I wasn't too convinced, however, and a few nights later when we happened to arrive at Harrah's at the same time, I steered him through the kitchen on our way to the dressing rooms. They have those huge scales there geared to weigh a side of beef or a couple of barrels of pickles, and before Barney knew what was happening, he was on the scales and watching in fascinated horror as the needle shot up to two hundred and thirty-five pounds. There was dead silence for a moment and then Barney, never at a loss for words, said in a small voice, "I've got my heavy shoes on tonight, Boss."

Well, we surmounted that little crisis, and Barney managed to get some of the extra poundage off, but over the next few years it kept creeping up, up, up. Jim Hobson complained that he couldn't get a good picture of him in the trombone section with all his extra chins and jowls, and I kept after him to reduce. Barney kept promising. But then he'd come face to face with some homemade bread, or a piece of fudge cake, or something equally tempting, and up he'd go another few pounds. Things came to a head a few years later when he hit an all-time high, and couldn't or wouldn't get his weight down. Finally, in desperation, I gave him his notice.

It was a very hard thing for me to do, but it was the only thing I could think of to impress him with the gravity of the situation. Barney was absolutely crushed and kept begging me to reconsider, and, for the first time in my life, so did the rest of the band. Almost every other musician in the orchestra came to me and asked me to give Barney another chance. "He's such a good fellow," I heard over and over. "He really does try, and he's a fine musician, and he has the best heart in the world."

I knew all that, which was one reason I'd already kept him on so long. But I felt both for Barney's sake and the morale of the band, that I had to take a firm stand.

But the pleasant pressure from the band continued, and Barney himself came and asked for one more chance. "I promise you I'll get my weight down," he said quietly. "I *promise* you, Boss!" Finally I said, "Well, Barney, I haven't hired anyone else to take your place. Why don't we try it for a while and see how things work out."

Next week Barney appeared for rehearsal, neat, clean, trim, determined . . . and a few pounds lighter. "Looka here, Boss," he said, pulling out his belt and sticking a couple of fingers inside his waistband. "See how much I've lost?" I nodded, impressed. Next week he bounded in looking more determined than ever. "Now take a look at *this*, Boss!" he said, jamming his whole hand inside his belt. "See here? A good two inches!" "Very good, Barney," I said. "Let's try it for another couple of weeks." For the next two weeks Barney concentrated on his diet and at the end of that time he came striding into rehearsal with a huge, triumphant grin on his face, just beaming. "Okay, Boss," he said, "Look at *this!*" And he doubled up his big fist . . . and it really is a big one! . . . and stuck it inside his belt. There was room to spare. I nodded, really impressed. He had not only slimmed down tremendously, he looked younger and handsomer. There was a new spring in his step, a sparkle in his eye. I looked at him for a moment and then I said, "Okay Barney. You've proved you could do it. You keep this up—and the job is yours."

Well, Barney is a sentimental man and so am I, and I think we both had a few tears in our eyes as he wrung my hand and nodded gruffly, not trusting himself to speak. A few weeks later we were able to present him with a stereo radio on the show, in honor of his twenty-fifth anniversary with us, and Barney really did break down that night. It meant a lot to all of us to still be together after a few tough setbacks. But the nicest moment of all, for me, came after the show when Barney said, "Boss, the greatest favor you ever did for me was to fire me. I just didn't realize how much I'd let myself go, what kind of shape I was really in. I was killing myself. So, with all my heart, I want to thank you."

I don't know if Barney realizes even now that it was just as hard on me to let him go as it was on him. I certainly didn't want to lose him . . . we'd spent a quarter of a century together—he was like a kid brother to me. But I knew he couldn't go on the way he was without destroying himself, and so I took the firm stand I did, and today Barney and I are closer pals than ever.

Our whole system works that way. It's based on caring—on investing love and hope in the other person and trying to help him become the best he can. And to me . . . and I think to all of us . . .that's the greatest success, the greatest joy, in the world.

PART THREE

ANOTHER DREAM

10

ANOTHER DREAM

I BEGAN WORKING MORE and more on my book in the latter half of the year. I wrote reams of copy on my yellow legal-sized tablets, trying to get my deepest beliefs, the principles which had been such a source of comfort to me, down on paper. I also kept trying to write a satisfactory outline of our Plan, but it kept eluding me, frustrating me. In addition, I read constantly, devouring the words of men far more able than I to put thoughts into words. Night after night I worked till very late, and I wondered, myself, at the urgency with which I did so. Why was I working so hard? Why was I pushing myself so? I didn't really know, but I felt impelled to keep going. Bernice came over very often so I could explain how I felt on certain issues and discuss the philosophies which had shaped and formed my life.

One night I got out my little prayer book to show her, the one my sister Eva had given me years before. There was my name on the flyleaf, L. Welk, and the date,

1927. I was twenty-four years old when she gave it to me, and it had a profound influence on my life. I think you can tell that just by looking at it . . . the maroon leather binding faded and worn, all the pages thumb-marked and underlined. I'm the kind of fellow who underlines passages meaningful to me and writes page numbers on the flyleaf so I'll know just where to find them. I still look through that little book. It's called *The Man of God,* and in addition to prayers, it contains pages and pages of the axioms and maxims which used to be such a big part of everybody's life.

"Kind words are the music of the world, and politeness its polish."

"All pleasures are deadly which are not in harmony with God's commandments."

"The resourceful man is one who, when he cannot do something one way, does it another."

And the one that stuck in my mind and has been so very helpful to me over the years: "No one is good for everything. Everyone is good for something. Do your bit, and do it well."

That little piece of advice had given me great comfort in my early years when I couldn't seem to do anything very well! I couldn't speak English, I blushed and stammered whenever I met anyone new, I couldn't look anybody in the eye—my list of drawbacks seemed endless. But I could play the accordion. I did have a thorough grounding in the love of God and family. I had complete faith in God. And I had big dreams. As it turned out, that was enough. Because I was fortunate enough to meet a man named George T. Kelly who

helped me take pride in the things I could do . . . and
work on the things I couldn't.

Mr. Kelly had a small traveling theatrical troupe,
and while we may not have made it on Broadway, we
were a smash hit in the small inland towns of the
Dakotas. That is, George was a smash success with his
comedy routines. I mainly went along to play for the
dances which followed the show. But George didn't let
me stop with that. He and his wife, Alma, spent hours
helping me learn English and develop stage presence
and . . . most important of all . . . believe in myself. He
told me over and over again what a good accordion
player I was—that I could be one of the best in the
world.

And as my self-confidence improved, so did my
playing. His ideas and theories made such an impression on me that unconsciously I used them all my life.
I don't suppose George ever dreamt that some of the
talks we had in those wee little towns, and some of the
ways he shared with me, would later be transformed
into our own System, which would not only change
the lives of the kids on our show, but also touch the
lives of millions of others through our music. His kindness, wisdom, and generosity have most certainly lived
on far beyond his scope of time and place.

George had taken me right off the farm—awkward,
shy, saddled with a giant inferiority complex, but burn-
ing with hopes and ambitions—and with kindness and
compassion, transformed my life. He had given me the
chance I needed, at the time in life I needed it so
desperately. Suddenly I understood, for the very first
time, just why I'd been working so hard. Because I was
trying to do for other young people exactly what George
had done for me! I was trying to open the door for

them, teach them what I had learned, help them step forward into life. *That's* why I was working so hard . . . for our young people.

I thought about it more and more in the next few weeks. I'd see little Mary Lou sailing through a dance number with delicate precision, or Tanya sparkling through a specialty song with Bob Havens or Henry Cuesta, or Sandi singing the lead in our trio. And I'd wonder . . . if we hadn't taken the time and effort to help them develop their talents . . . what would have happened? It had taken us a while to discover that Mary Lou had great natural talent as a dancer, that Tanya did so well with rhythm numbers, and that Sandi could sing a solo! Sandi, in particular, had found herself in a tough spot when her singing partner, Salli, left the show in 1972 to try for a career of her own. We weren't quite sure what to do about her, and as Sandi herself later confessed, she'd shed a few tears in private, wondering the same thing. "I knew you were overloaded with singers," she told me, "so I didn't know what you could do with me alone. After all, you'd hired me as part of a team." Well, I didn't know myself for a while. But Sandi is such a wonderful person and has such fine qualities. She's one of the finest ladies I've ever known, and I knew we had to figure out some way to keep her.

Finally, I suggested she team with Mary Lou and Gail. I really didn't expect too much, because the best singing groups are almost always composed of members of the same family. As a rule, they share the same general physical traits and, consequently, come up with a closer blend. But these three lovely ladies really surprised me! They worked together with such zeal they came up with a unique blend all their own. Sandi began singing more and more of the solo lines in their songs, and as the trio improved, so did she.

So when we went to Tahoe in 1974, I decided to entrust her with a solo spot of her own, a beautiful song called, "And I Love You So." I had a little resistance from some of my right-hand people who thought she wasn't quite ready. But I was so sold on her that for once I decided to override them. I don't think anyone who saw that show will ever forget the way Sandi stepped out from the wings into the glow of a single spotlight, wearing a flowing violet chiffon gown, with her long red hair streaming down her back, and then walked slowly across the stage, singing with such feeling, such warmth, she captured everyone's heart. We got quite a bonus out of that entire situation. We not only helped Sandi develop into a solo performer, we also came up with a brand new trio which has since become one of our most popular features. Many of our fans have told us the girls have one of the best blends they've ever heard.

Looking back over the years, I could remember several other performers we'd helped develop . . . little Bobby Beers, who was with me in the pre-television days; Bob Ralston; Buddy Merrill; the Lennon sisters. Janet Lennon had been only nine-and-a-half when we found her, and she and her sisters had grown up on the show in full view of the whole nation, who looked on fondly as we trained them. The girls had happily stayed with us for twelve years, and then gone on to a successful career of their own . . . so I knew our ideas worked very well with young people. The real problem that faced us was in being allowed to work with them! The child labor laws and other restrictions and expenses made it nearly impossible.

One night I sat down and made a list of all the

reasons I could think of, both for and against young people working at an early age. I could think of a dozen for doing so . . . but none for not working! On the plus side, I wrote: "Allowing a young person to work freely would give him a chance to try different jobs; find a profession to his liking; get the training he needs at no cost whatsoever; earn while he learns; learn how to get along with people; visualize future goals; develop qualities of self-reliance and initiative; learn the attributes that build strong character; and learn all these things at the time in life when it is easiest and best." That last point was such a strong one, in my opinion. Most everyone agrees that we learn physical skills better when we're young. But the same thing holds true for mental skills and character development . . . and I had a whole orchestra full of examples to prove my point: Myron Floren learned to play the accordion when he was only about five; I myself learned to play the pump organ when I was four, and the accordion not long afterward; Cissy King was dancing at the age of three (can't you just see Cissy spinning around on her toes at that age?); Charlotte Harris could play the piano at three and the cello at five; Bob Ralston was already a piano virtuoso at the age of fifteen; Ralna English was singing before she could talk. ("My mother told me I would come toddling around the corner of the house singing at the top of my lungs before I could even talk . . . and could barely walk!" she confided). All of them learned their skills early, early in life; and, more importantly, they had also learned the character traits that propelled them into success.

Early training has a fundamental, lifelong effect. I'm convinced that we can help our young people most by helping them get started as young as humanly possible, and creating in them a desire to make a mark in the

world . . . on their own. As it is, they're often coddled
and protected by their parents (or the schools . . . or
the government) to such an extent that they're led,
almost encouraged, to become dependent. Worse, they
are actually prevented from shouldering the responsibilities that can help them grow and develop the most.
No wonder they lose their natural enthusiasm and initiative, and soon acquire an apathetic "I don't care"
attitude. Young folks should really "hunger" to make
something of themselves, and giving them a chance to
work at an early age is one of the best ways to do so.

There was still another reason I'd like to see young
people given a chance to work: With young people
around me all the time, I was aware of their tremendous energy, their enormous vitality. I have a lot
of stamina myself, but there were some days at the
studio when I realized vividly what a big difference
there is between seventy and seventeen, not to mention
seven! Young people sometimes seem almost to boil
over with creative energy, and I knew that if we didn't
help them channel it into constructive outlets, it could
spill over into destructive ones. There's an old saying,
so old I can recall hearing my parents say it to me,
"Now remember, little Lawrence, 'Idle hands are the
Devil's workshop!' "—and in my experience, I have
found that to be certainly true. It's when youngsters
have time on their hands and can't get a job, that the
world around them seems to lose its meaning, and they
fall easy prey to temptation. I'm reasonably certain
that if we had allowed and encouraged our young people to get involved with productive jobs over the past
thirty or forty years, we wouldn't have many of the
problems which face us today. I'm equally certain we'd
be doing our young people a tremendous favor if we

could only find a way to amend the child labor laws, and give our young folks a chance to work.

It's not that I want to force them to work! I just want to free their hands and give them the privilege of working—if they want to.

I imagine that most of us would agree the child labor laws were passed originally in an attempt to protect our youngsters from unscrupulous employers; and that was certainly an admirable intention. But somehow those laws backfired, creating the conditions we have today. And instead of punishing the offending employer, as they were meant to do, these restrictions ended up "punishing" the children, by making it very difficult for them to get a job. I realize of course, that it *is* possible to get work permits, under certain conditions. But very few employers have either the time, patience or the stamina to contend with all the necessary red tape and regulations. The result is our young folks lose their chances to learn through work. The more I thought about it, the more I felt they were entitled to those chances.

At the same time, I knew that getting the labor laws changed would be a tremendous undertaking, practically an impossibility in our increasingly regimented society. But nobody has yet accused me of being practical! Idealistic, maybe. Optimistic, yes. And determined, absolutely! "I may not be able to make much of a dent in my own lifetime," I told Ted Lennon one day, discussing this situation, "but perhaps I can sow a seed. Perhaps I can get folks to see the truth of what I feel so deep in my heart, so that someday, they will bring those changes about."

Meanwhile . . . until that period *someday* came along . . . I stuck to business as usual, working with all our kids. As I mentioned, we had decided to assign

Gail to the Semonskis, to write arrangements for them and help coach them, and it was making a big difference. Each week Gail would work out a special arrangement of their song, take it out to their house, and work with them for half an hour or so. A couple of days later, she'd go back and work with them again for another forty minutes or an hour; by the time we were ready to tape the show, the girls had had a very good chance to learn their song.

It was beginning to show results. Even George said rather grudgingly one day, "Well, I've gotta admit it, they're getting better. For one thing, they're not as scared as they were—they have a lot more poise. And since we've 'placed' their voices (put them in the range best suited to them) their sound is a whole lot better. You may be right, Lawrence. They may make it after all."

There was no doubt whatever that they had all learned to face the cameras with more ease and grace. Watching them walk confidently onstage, stepping over the huge coiled cables in their path, and then group themselves prettily in front of the massive lights and cameras, their father suddenly turned to me and said, "Mr. Welk, our girls have learned more here in the past few months than they ever could have learned in any school —anywhere, anytime, anyplace. Rusty and I will be forever grateful to you."

Naturally, I was pleased at his nice words but, strangely enough, I felt a little letdown, too. Because I knew that what we were doing for the Semonskis could be done for dozens more youngsters . . . thousands, really . . . if only things weren't so rigidly controlled. For years I'd dreamed of starting little orchestras in every city and town in the nation, so young kids could learn their profession by actually playing for church clubs and home parties. And then as they improved, they could move on up into the "big time" . . . something like the farm system used in baseball. It seemed like an eminently feasible idea to me, but I was constantly being told it was impossible, just a dream.

Well, maybe so. But I'd had a lot of other impossible dreams in my day and watched a good many of them come true. And so I filed this latest dream at the back of my mind along with all the others, where I could think about them and do what I could to make them come true.

And meanwhile—just to help things along—I kept right on working!

11

FAMILIES

WHENEVER WE MADE UNUSUALLY good progress with any of our newcomers, I was almost sure to find they'd already had a good home life. In fact, one of the things that was helping us so much with the Semonski girls was the fact that their parents had given us pretty good material to start with! The girls may have been totally unprofessional and in·need of intensive training, but their basic good character and wholesomeness gave them a tremendous advantage. It always does. I remember when Ralna first joined us—she was just so talented and professional there was very little for us to do. And also, she was so cooperative and dependable she was an absolute joy to have around. I suspected at once she'd had a very good upbringing, and she had! When we played her hometown of Lubbock, Texas, a year later, I met her whole family—mother, father, sisters, uncles, aunts, cousins, neighbors, friends—they all showed up, and you could just see how very loved Ralna was by all of them. Afterward, they put on a big party for her and it was oustanding in several respects. For one thing, you could actually hear yourself talk! . . . something pretty unusual for the average noisy show-business party. For another, they served home-baked cookies, cakes, and other goodies and served milk and coffee instead of liquor (just my cup of tea, I might add). The whole atmosphere was so close, so warm, so full of relaxed easy laughter and good humor, it was easy to see where Ralna had learned her "hominess" and high standards.

Sandi has a background much like that, and so do Mary Lou, Tanya, and Gail . . . in fact, nearly all our people come from close families. And for the few in our Musical Family who don't, our family itself helps give them what they missed.

I believe in families. I wouldn't be calling our group today a Musical Family if I didn't. I sensed the strength of a good family even during my earliest days on the farm when I was hopelessly convinced that I was the *dummer-esel* of all time. (And with good reason, I might add! I was small, skinny, and so shy I turned scarlet if anybody spoke to me.) But even then my mother gave me such love, such unquestioning devotion that I felt absolutely secure. My father, too, although constantly exasperated by my fumbling attempts to help him with his blacksmith and other chores, truly did love me and I knew it. And to see him and my mother strolling around our farm together, hand in hand, admiring the fields, making plans for the future, always deferring to each other's wishes, always together, was a lesson in love for all of us. I don't recall either my father or mother ever telling me how to build a happy marriage. But in a family, you live with people who are models for your life . . . and my parents gave us a wonderful example.

I've been so lucky in my own family life. Over and

over again I've realized how fortunate I was to find Fern. When others tell us how well our three children turned out, it is always easy for me to give Fern the credit. I love my children with all my heart and always have, and I've done the best I could to provide for them and be a good father, but Fern has been the heart and soul of our home. She was the one who held everything together when I had to be out on the road, the one who made it so warm and pleasant and inviting that I was always more than anxious to get back. If she had been a different kind of person, one who put a career above her role as wife and mother—how very different our lives would have been!

On Father's Day a year or so ago, my daughter Donna wrote me a letter. I was in Tahoe at the time with our Musical Family, and I read the letter in my dressing room that evening between shows, with the doors closed and the happy hubbub in the hallway outside sounding through faintly. Donna recalled incidents from her childhood, and the excitement she felt when I was coming home from trips. "Larry, Shirley, and I would be up in the tree," she wrote, "and we'd hear your car coming down the street, and we'd plop down out of the tree like overripe cherries, racing to see who could get to you first!" She remembered the stories I used to tell her, the little "in" jokes that every family shares, the "discussions" that made her "gulp"! "Whenever I heard you say, 'Donna, may I have a word with you, please?' I knew another lecture was coming!" But then she went on to write how very much those lectures had helped her in raising her own three children. I loved that letter and tried to read it aloud to a friend, but I finally gave up and just handed it over. Donna's letter may not have been a masterpiece of writing, but the warmth, the consideration, the love that shows through, makes it something I'll always treasure.

We have a tradition in our family, started by our daughter Shirley, of sharing holidays and birthdays together and having everyone . . . even the very smallest person present . . . write little letters and notes to the honored guest. By now we have several books filled with such letters, including a few scrawled by two-year-old hands, which aren't too easy to understand but are very meaningful! I particularly enjoyed one note from Jon, Shirley's middle boy, who wrote, "Dear Grandpa, I hope you have a happy Father's Day and I hope you have a happy year and I hope we can have lunch together soon. Love, Jon . . . . P.S. This time, lunch is on me." Coming from a Welk, as that one did, I felt it was proof positive he loved me!

I often think of what a friend of mine said to me years ago. He was a business acquaintance whom I had met shortly after coming to California in the fifties, and he was fabulously wealthy, a super-success, judged by most standards. I invited him home to dinner with us one night, and we shared a simple meal together, one that seemed almost out of keeping with his luxurious standard of living. But when he left at the end of the evening, he turned to me . . . this man who apparently had everything life had to offer . . . and with tears in his eyes, said, "Lawrence, I want to tell you something. I'd give everything I have, every penny I possess, if I could have a family like yours. You have everything."

There is nothing quite like the love you receive in a family. In most cases you are loved for yourself alone and given the warmth and constant care that help you grow and develop. When I was a child, the family was still the center of life, the unquestioned basic social unit, the place where you learned the fundamental moral and ethical laws to carry you through life. Your relationship to your family was the most powerful influence of all in forming your character. Throughout history the family has always been a most stable and consistent force for good in any established human society.

But today, families are under attack from all sides. They're getting smaller, breaking apart, disappearing completely. People are beginning to live more and more for themselves . . . and loneliness has become our national illness.

I'm afraid many people today have just lost touch with the simple joys of family life . . . with that feeling of unity, of belonging, of plain comforting love for each other. We need it. Not long ago I bundled up a whole group of my grandchildren . . . there were about fourteen of us, counting mothers and assorted friends . . . and we all went off to the circus. We were all sizes and ages, ranging from seventy-two (me) to two-and-a-half (Kevin, Tanya and Larry's young son). And we all sat in the front row and laughed at the clowns, applauded the trapeze performers, cheered the animal acts, and got stiff necks looking at the high-wire act directly overhead. And afterward, we all drove off for hamburgers and foot-long hot dogs, and then drove on to Clancy Muldoon's on Wilshire Boulevard for ice cream cones. By that time, the little ones were daubed from head to foot with ice cream, some of the mothers were beginning to wilt—and Grandpa had *had* it! But I wouldn't have missed that outing for the world. There is just no love like family love, no joy like family joy, that unique combination of pride in each other's achievements, and loving understanding of each other's shortcomings.

I can still see my own mother . . . always so neat

and clean . . . her hair curling slightly around her face, her eyes very blue, very clear, always busy, but never too busy to hug us or let us know she cared. My mother listened to our dreams, encouraged us, and gave us her absolute, unwavering, complete love. It was enough to last a lifetime.

No teacher, however fine, can replace a dedicated mother. A small child who is denied the kind of selfless love a real mother provides can never quite overcome that handicap. Studies show that infants can actually die if there is no one to love them, and hold them, and cuddle them. There is a need in the human spirit for complete love—love that asks nothing in return, love that is freely given from a source more divine than human—the kind of love God gives to us . . . and the kind a mother gives her child. Nothing can replace it nor even approximate it. And if the world loses that, we have lost an irreplaceable treasure.

12

MY TEAM

THE SEMONSKIS WERE IMPROVING steadily—there was just no doubt about it. They were doing things of their own volition more and more, and all of us were pleased —especially me! I'd been pretty worried during the summer months that they were just not going to make it, but now I was very, very hopeful they would. (Nevertheless, I prudently decided not to make a firm decision until I was absolutely sure!)

It was of enormous satisfaction to me to realize that it was our System that was helping them so much. It wasn't me—or at least it wasn't me alone. It was my right-hand people who had pitched in so wholeheartedly to help. George Cates and Bob Ballard had probably done the most to get the girls off on the right foot —finding the best range for them to sing in, teaching them how to "phrase" and "breathe" and even how close to stand to the microphone, all of which were of vital importance and about which the girls knew absolutely nothing. Curt Ramsey and Jack Imel had been of great help, giving them pointers on how to walk and stand onstage. Jim Hobson had put his genius-mind to work experimenting with different camera angles and, as the months went by, he and Jack and their assistant, Doug Smart, began to come up with production ideas and sets which gave the girls' songs much more life and color. Duane Fulcher advised them about simple make-up and hair styles; Rose Weiss designed youthful, flattering costumes; Les Kaufman, our publicity chief, gave them helpful information about public relations. Everybody helped, but I think little Gail was perhaps the biggest help of all, searching tirelessly for exactly the right songs to suit their youth and talent and then writing the simple, catchy arrangements which showed them off the best. It was really the fifty family talents in our group that were helping the girls so much. Everybody was joining forces just the way you do in a real family to show off your newest members to their best advantage.

And something else was helping them, too, and that was the hand of "family" friendship being extended to them. Joe Feeney with his big brood of ten children was a natural, I suppose, to become one of their closest friends. Tanya, our resident "hostess," was one of the first to invite them to her home. Norma gave them her diet and health tips. Everyone tried to make them feel welcome. Even our stage crew got into the act. As they came to know the girls better, they, too, became allied in the fight to help them make it. And that open, warm, friendly encouragement on all sides was almost as important to the girls' development as the actual professional coaching they were getting, maybe more so.

We've always had that wonderful friendliness in our group. One of the things that astonishes others in the world of entertainment is the lack of jealousy among our people. Oh, of course, there's a little—there's bound to be—that's just human nature. And occasionally when one of our people hears another singing just the song he wanted to sing, he's a little unhappy about it. And there may be a certain amount of apprehension whenever anyone new is brought into the show . . . again, that's only natural. But it's a minor reaction, very minor, and seems to vanish very quickly. By and large there is such a lack of jealousy it's amazing . . . especially among the girls, where you might expect to find more of it. But in our case, it's just the opposite. All kinds of examples spring to mind . . . Cissy offering to cut one of her dance numbers at Tahoe so "Mary Lou can have a chance"; Tanya offering to turn her solo into a duet so Anacani would have a spot on the show; and all the girls standing together in the wings at Tahoe listening intently to Ralna sing her number and then cheering and applauding louder than the audience when Ralna earned herself a standing ovation. The girls seem honestly to rejoice in each other's success. They know . . . we all know . . . the better the show, the better for us. And when you keep that firmly in mind, it puts everything into the proper perspective.

I don't say that every time we bring someone new on the show there is an instantaneous show of friendship. It takes time to grow, just as it does in a real family. But it is there . . . ready to be offered, ready to grow.

And it makes me so proud of our kids! Proud of their goodness, proud of their talents, proud of the way they represent us when they make appearances on their own. Sometimes people say to me, "How can you let your stars go out alone and earn money for themselves on others shows?" Well, if they can, I'm delighted! If being on our show helps them get appearances at fairs and concerts—wonderful! It only helps us, because every time one of our people—Henry Cuesta, Myron Floren, or one of our talented singers—goes out and makes a nice impression on the audience, he helps all the rest of us back home. Their triumphs are our triumphs. We are honestly proud of them. Again, that's our Family System in action. And that was what was helping the Semonskis most of all.

Of course, every day was a learning experience for them—for all of us really. Sometimes as I myself worked with them, pointing out some little thing they may not have noticed otherwise, I'd remember the lessons George Kelly had taught me without my even knowing it. Just being with him, listening to his bubbling Irish personality, as he charmed people over the phone setting up our bookings, watching his courtly manners, noting his unfailing habit of always looking on the pleasant side of any situation . . . all those things rubbed off on me and helped me later on in life. It made me realize again how powerful are the lessons we learn when we are young. We never quite forget them. Like the time I learned the hard way never to overstay my welcome!

I was about nineteen and on my way to play at a dance in Zeeland, North Dakota, a couple of hours away by train from Strasburg. We had one train a day in those years. It came through in the morning and returned again in the late afternoon, and it was always the high spot of the day. I boarded it, full of excitement, and we started off down the track toward Zeeland.

There were a couple of salesmen in our coach who knew me from some of the dances I'd played in the area, and they asked me if I'd favor them with a few tunes. Would I! I didn't have to be asked twice, and I leaped for my accordion case, got out my accordion, pulled the straps over my shoulders, and started in. Now I may not have played too well at the time but I did play loud. One of the main things I'd learned at barn dances was to play loudly enough so the dancers could hear me over the general hilarity which always took over as the schnapps began to take effect. So now I played with all stops out—waltzes, polkas, schottisches, old-country folk tunes, wedding dances—I even threw in a couple of marches. I was having an absolutely wonderful time!

At Hague, the train stopped to pick up a few more passengers and take on some water from the water tower, and my friends rushed out to the platform to get some fresh air—and probably a little relief! When they returned, they told me they'd decided to get up a card game and they pressed me to join them. "Oh, that's all right," I said, not getting their point at all. "I like to play the accordion!" And I burst into my favorite waltz, "Over the Waves." Suddenly one of the fellows threw down his cards, grabbed great hunks of his hair in both hands, and shouted, "Please! Please, please, *please* stop it, Lawrence! It was all right to start with, but I just can't *stand* any more!" Crushed and humiliated beyond belief, I put my accordion away immediately and sat all by myself for the rest of the trip. It was a harsh lesson —it really did hurt my feelings—but a good one, and I never forgot it. (It's one of the reasons we try to keep our show moving as fast as possible today!) And whenever any of our people gets so carried away by the audience response he wants to run right back onstage and do a few more encores, I always remember that train trip to Zeeland and I say, "Well, I really wouldn't advise that. Always leave your audience wanting a little bit more. Never overstay your welcome."

That's not only a good rule for show business. That's a pretty good rule for life.

13

EDUCATION

WE TEACH THROUGH A combination of love, encouragement, and example. Love—an honest concern for the other person—has always been an unparalleled way to develop people, of course. But encouragement is of vital importance, too.

So when any of our kids takes a step forward, no matter how small, I make it a point to compliment and encourage him. I learned a long time ago that a well-placed word of praise can motivate far better than criticism. I'd say the key word is "positive." We try always to stay on the positive side.

And I've always believed that simply *believing* in someone can be the best way in the world to encourage him. Everything has to start in the mind first . . . it has to happen there. If you believe in someone else's talents strongly enough, pretty soon he'll begin to believe, too, and the results can be nothing short of miraculous. (It works on yourself, too. All my life, I've set up a goal, a dream, and then I believe, with absolute confidence, that I'll make it. And so many times I do. In fact, my daughter Donna once said thoughtfully, "You know, Dad, we Welks aren't so talented. Just persistent!" She has a point.)

More than anything else, we teach by example. I can't very well ask my people to be honest, trustworthy, loyal—and on time—if I don't at least try to be that way myself. I doubt if any us ever told the Semonskis to be punctual at rehearsals, but when they saw everybody else in the group not only on time, but early—they got the message. When they saw Norma Zimmer flawlessly groomed at all times, her songs thoroughly prepared; Tom Netherton equally immaculate and always with a friendly smile; Myron constantly practicing his accordion technique off in the corner; Anacani speaking easily and fluently in two different languages and always so willing and anxious to work; Jim Hobson with his temper firmly under control in spite of the inevitable goof-ups that occur from time to time—it made a tremendous impression on them. Jim is a wonderful example, a wonderful teacher. I tell him he's the only man I know who can correct other people and be loved for it! He does it so smoothly, so gently, that no one is hurt.

Actually, we teach from life, from experience . . . and I'm convinced that practical experience is the best education there is. Of course, I hope you folks realize how much nerve it takes for me to talk about education! After all, I never got beyond the fourth grade because of illness, and for years I was miserably self-conscious over that fact. I was always a little embarrassed and ill at ease whenever I was around people who had more education than I—which was practically all the time. But gradually I realized that education is not a matter of degrees or diplomas. It doesn't stop short when you graduate. Education is a lifelong process, and whenever you work on yourself—learning new things, reading, growing, developing whatever potential you have to the highest possible degree—you are educating yourself. That's the basic principle behind the kind of teaching and education we give our kids.

Not long ago I read an article by a famous educator in Northern California and I got so excited I practically flew up to talk to him personally! What impressed me was that he said, in much better words than I, that one of the worst things we can do to our children is to bar them from working. You can't make a good man out of a boy if you don't let him learn the discipline and power of work in his early years, he said, and went on to add that the child labor laws and wage restrictions were hurting young people far more than they were helping. I agree with him completely. I've had friends who said, emphatically, that their children would never have to work as hard as they did. "I have money now and I can afford to give my children a good life," they say. But you can't *give* life to anyone. It has to be earned.

That's why we set up goals for our younger kids and let them work toward them on their own. We're there to help, to encourage, to give as good an example as we can . . . to love. But they have to do it on their own. And the Semonskis were learning that little by little and day by day.

14

BICENTENNIAL PRAYER

I WAS FILLED WITH unusual energy as we swung into high gear, winding up all our projects. I always seem to have a lot of vitality. I remember one time I was being interviewed for a newspaper article, and I was rattling off my schedule of the previous week, when the reporter sighed deeply and put down his pencil. "Mr. Welk," he said, shaking his head, "I'm half your age, but I'm getting tired just listening to you!"

Well, I do believe in action. I've been that way all my life. In my younger days I never walked, always ran, and I'm still pretty much that way . . . only now I don't trot quite as fast as I used to! But to me, life *is* action— and you have to plunge in and do things to make it satisfactory. And do things not just for yourself but for others—speak to them (and speak to them first), smile, offer to help, share yourself a little bit. I can tell you from personal experience, your life will be twice as happy. I marvel at my happiness today. I seem to be surrounded by love and affection on all sides, and, apart from being singularly blessed by God, I can only surmise it's a kind of return on whatever love and affection I've tried to give others throughout my life. That's part of my basic philosophy, "Give and it shall be given unto you." It works just as completely in matters of the spirit as in economics or anything else.

Sometimes I'm afraid people will think I speak only of the good things in our lives, that everything is just sweetness and light with us. But, of course, that's not the case. Life isn't like that, and we have our low spots, our dark times, our discouraging days. The whole nation knew about it the day we got fired! Still, it's true that for the most part we stay pretty much on the positive side, and I give full credit for it to our System. What else could it be?

Some of my happiest moments come when I watch our show at home on Saturday night in our music room. Fern is always there, of course, and sometimes Bernice as we worked on the book. We often broke into applause when one of the kids did an especially good job or the band sounded better than usual. (Except Fern! She appreciates it but, as she says with complete logic, "Why should I applaud? They can't hear me!") But I do, anyway. In fact, I do everything but stand up and cheer when I think the kids do something especially well.

Our Bicentennial Show affected me that way. We did it in two parts, as some of you may remember. During the first show I was lying on the divan at home watching it . . . and six different times during that show, the hair just stood right up on my arms. I was just covered with gooseflesh (I guess my goosebumps are my own personal barometer of how good a thing is!) But I was so moved when Norma and Jim Roberts sang "Will You Remember?" from *Maytime*. It brought back memories of the days when I, myself, first had dreams of breaking into show business. And looking at Norma, so radiant and lovely, realizing she had been with us for sixteen years, made me so grateful for the privilege of knowing her and having had her with us all those years. There were other "goosebump" times . . . Henry Cuesta and the band doing "Rhapsody in Blue" with Bob Smale playing such sensational jazz runs in the background I was absolutely dazzled. How finely developed the two of them are! The boys in the band made me proud of them with a medley from *Show Boat* and a group of Stephen Foster tunes. And there were other moments . . . Tom, Mary Lou, and the girls doing a tribute to Hawaii, with Mary Lou dancing a graceful hula and Tom singing as well as I've ever heard him; the whole group doing the Charleston sparked by our incomparable Bobby and Cissy: and I was especially moved by our two closing numbers, "The Battle Hymn of the Republic" on the first show and "America the Beautiful" on the second—just filled with pride and gratitude and wonder at how well these people, my kids, had developed themselves. In fact, it seems to me that I'm actually more in the business of developing people than developing an orchestra! You can't do one without the other, of course, but it's the human element that fascinates me most. My daughter Shirley once said, "Dad, if you hadn't become a musician, you'd have made a great psychologist. You're always trying to figure out what makes people tick." She's right. At least she's right about my wanting to know what makes people tick. Human behavior has always fascinated me, and I think it's probably the most underdeveloped field we have. We've learned how to put a man on the moon and get to the bottom of the sea, but we haven't learned about our own emotions, our own motivations.

But I had learned a few things which I knew from

experience were of tremendous help in developing people. I'd learned, for example, that if you expect the best from a person, he will almost always give it to you. If you treat others fairly and with compassion and generosity, that's the kind of treatment you'll get back. The basics, the unchanging principles of human behavior, do work, and I tried hard to convey all these ideas to the people in my care . . . the necessity for being sensitive to other people's needs, of understanding the value of honest work, preparation, humility, compassion, and gratitude. Simply gratitude seems to have vanished from our lives. We take so many of our daily wonders completely for granted. All the laborsaving devices, all the light and power and warmth, all the marvels of communication and transportation. Even in Los Angeles we take things like automobiles for granted, and yet we really couldn't live without them.

Zooming around a corner one day it suddenly occurred to me that I hadn't had car trouble in years. I hadn't even had a flat tire . . . and it made me remember the time in Yankton, South Dakota, when I first had a little band and I had four blowouts in one day! I'd bought a set of brand new tires, put them all on my car, and then the whole band—six of us, plus our instruments—crowded in. The tires just couldn't take it and one after another they exploded! I spent most of that day underneath the car, wrestling with a wrench and a jack, changing tires and patching inner tubes; and if I'd been a swearing man I'd have certainly let loose with a few choice words that might have ruined the boys! I really can't tell you how I felt when I heard the fourth tire go flat. What a day! But the point is, we take such perfection as fine tires and cars completely for granted. Both Fern and I drive Dodge cars and have for years. Not because Dodge was our first sponsor, but because they're so troublefree, so wonderful. But, like everyone else, we take their perfection for granted.

It isn't just our material advantages we overlook, it's our spiritual ones, too. Because in spite of our inflation, crime rates, and other serious problems, this is *still* the greatest nation in the world. We still have a certain amount of freedom, we can still go to bed at night without concern that the secret police will pound on our doors, we can still speak freely, still worship as we please. There are many countries in the world where this is not possible.

I'm afraid we've forgotten what we owe to our forefathers. Just as we should be thanking those who invented the electric light, the telephone, television, and so on, so too should we be thanking those who gave us things far more important—the right to live freely, to worship God, to raise our children as we see fit. Those are tremendous gifts which can never be paid for in dollars and cents—only through the full use of the potentials God gave us, only in ways that will serve Him best.

Someone once said that our freedom was not bought and paid for in one installment at Valley Forge—it is a lifetime obligation which has to be renewed every year. A little simple gratitude on our part would help to pay that debt. In fact, our hearts should be filled with gratitude as we approach our Bicentennial year! We are the oldest surviving democratic republic in history, and we have the greatest chance since time began to make our form of freedom endure. Other great civilizations have risen before ours, and there have been other governments based on the nobility and freedom of the human spirit. But none of them has endured as long as ours. And I am deeply, passionately proud that our nation has been able to do this.

The little Semonskis, when I first began training them at our mobile home in Escondido. That's Michelle on my lap, then JoAnne, Donna, Valerie, Diane, and Audrey. This was taken right after Christmas as you can see by the tree at the right. In the background is a figurine which the girls made as a gift for me. Each figure represents one of them.   *Leo North*

The Semonskis, one year later—well on their way. Audrey, Diane, and Donna are in the top row, with JoAnne, Michelle, and Valerie in front.   *Leo North*

George Cates, the man who brings out the best in "the boss" . . . by disagreeing with me from time to time! George knows what he is doing, and the band is richer and better because of him. *Tom Mareschal*

These two nice people really take their work seriously—always prepared, always dependable. It was truly a happy day for us when we found our wonderful young married couple, Guy and Ralna. *Leo North*

Arthur Duncan, the fine gentleman who is doing a tremendous job of keeping tap dancing alive in this country. Arthur also has a wonderful sense of humor. When you see and hear him on tour you'll know what I mean.   *Leo North*

Jack Imel (center) is not only a fine drummer, he's also a great tap dancer, a fine marimba player, a good singer—and the best assistant producer any show could ever have. A great talent. *Leo North*

Three of the "most beautiful girls in the world" as they looked during our show at Tahoe. No wonder I loved the opening of that show so much! Left to right, Sandi, Ralna, and Gail. *Leo North*

One of our most valuable members. Anacani was practically waiting for me on the doorstep of our restaurant in Escondido, when I happened to visit there one day. I hired her immediately as our singing hostess, and since that time she's become one of our most popular and best-loved performers, one we're all proud of.   *Leo North*

I'm so happy my good friends Harold and Sheila Schafer "pestered" me to give Tom Netherton a try-out, because he has become one of the most popular singers of all time on our show. Tom is six-foot-five, and just as fine a gentleman in person as he appears to be on television.   *Leo North*

Here's the Filipino "Tinickling" dance during which Cissy got her ankle caught by those heavy bamboo poles. She showed the kind of trouper she is when she went right into the next number without a break, and then insisted on doing the whole dance over again after the show was over. What a great trouper, and what a great lady!

And here's the whole band, resplendent in red, white, and blue costumes, with me holding the big bass drum, on stage at Harrah's at Tahoe just after our nightly march through the audience. *Harrah's, Tahoe*

Our country gal, Ava Barber, really knows how to sing a country song. And why not? She's from the heart of country music, Knoxville and Nashville, Tennessee. A lovely lady.
Leo North

Aren't they sweet? It always gives me such a warm feeling to see how our girls truly like each other, and welcome newcomers to the show. Here Tanya and Anacani share a song together, as they did when Anacani first joined our show.   *Leo North*

Bob Ralston and Charlotte Harris play the kind of classic songs which bring back memories of the days when such melodies were heard all the time, in homes and restaurants everywhere. Bob and Charlotte are such marvelous musicians, they never fail to please our audiences.   *Leo North*

I just thought I'd let you in on a picture which gives you some idea of the fun we have working on our show. Cissy and Mary Lou are two of my most favorite dancing partners.
Leo North

Nine of our "beauties," with part of our reed, string, and wood-wind sections. Left to right, top row, are Ava, Mary Lou, Tanya, Anacani, Norma, Gail, Ralna, Sandi, and Cissy. That's Harry Hyams at the viola, top left, then Joe Livoti, our first violinist, and singer-violinist Bob Lido. Bottom row are Dave Edwards, our first saxophonist, Bob Davis, another tremendous musician, and Henry Cuesta, our superlative clarinet soloist.
Leo North

Two long-time favorites of our fans, Norma Zimmer and Jim Roberts, singing "Will You Remember" from *Maytime,* on our Bicentennial special. Their complete dedication has helped our show so much. *Leo North*

Gail Farrell is the "junior member" and Larry Hooper the "senior partner" in our wonderful group of piano artists.
Leo North

My good friend Bill Breck is my host whenever I play in the Tucson, Arizona, Pro-Am golf tournament—and that always doubles my pleasure. And here I am, having even more fun on opening day, "waltzing" with one of the ladies from the gallery, with Joe Garagiola racing up to tag in!   *Jack Sheaffer*

With the famous and likable Patty Berg at the Dinah Shore-Colgate Women's Golf Tournament in Palm Springs, California. *Eddie Shipstad*

If you visit our place in Escondido, you'll see this fountain in the lake in front of the restaurant. My cousin Johnny Klein, who plays drums in the band, designed and built the fountain and presented it to us as a gift. Here relaxing in front of it are Guy, Larry Hooper, and Tom, with Ralna, Ava, and Norma in front.   *Leo North*

Fern and I inspecting the new buffet in our restaurant in Escondido, with manager, Paul Ryan, and our wonderful chef, Bill Balnaves. *Eddie Shipstad*

Aren't they a nice couple? Richard Maloof has always told me how grateful and happy he is to be with the band. I think Mary Lou must have something to do with that! Their wedding was a big event in our Musical Family.

Two of my favorite people on their wedding day, Lois and Russ Klein. Russ is a completely professional musician who has been with us for almost twenty years. Lois handles her job with great efficiency and makes many friends for us with her warm and friendly personality. *Leo North*

Our production staff found out a long time ago what lies close to my heart . . . the farm. So here are three of the prettiest girls you'll find on any farm, or anywhere else for that matter: Gail, Sandi, and Mary Lou. Aren't they pretty?   *Leo North*

Several of my closest friends and associates attended the ground-breaking ceremonies for our Lawrence Welk Plaza . . . you can see them in the background. And it was obvious to all of them I'd been away from the farm entirely too long, because I kept saying, "Giddyup horse, giddyup!" until finally one of my friends yelled, "Hey Lawrence—that horsie is a mule!"
Larry Lee Photography

And here it is . . . a long, long way from a small sod farm-house to this twenty-one-story office building (housing our offices), and an adjoining sixteen-story Champagne Towers apartment complex, at the corner of Ocean Avenue and Wilshire Boulevard, overlooking the Pacific Ocean in Santa Monica. Only in America could this be possible.

Here we are underway with our Plaza project, admiring a model of the projected office building. As you folks know, it was really the baton that got this whole thing started, so here I am holding one, alongside Ted Lennon, who took on the responsibility for the whole enterprise and still has it. On the other side of the model is my good friend and pal Parker Sullivan, president of the General Telephone Company, which occupies fifteen floors of the building, and T. K. Kutay, another partner in the project.
Larry Lee Photography

I like this picture of Bobby and Cissy. They're smiling and so is everybody else in the audience. Right behind Cissy's top-knot is Jack Lennon, an uncle of the Lennon sisters. *Leo North*

Yes . . . babies are always "Welkome" on our show! (I just couldn't resist that!) Here are Guy and Ralna admiring Sandi and Brent Griffiths' five-week-old son, Benjamin Brent Griffiths.

Joe Feeney, our great Irish tenor. When he hits one of those high notes . . . everybody applauds. Enthusiastically!
Leo North

Thought we'd show you two of our handsomest members
—way back when! When I first found Dick Dale, he was
with Harold Loeffelmacher's "Six Fat Dutchmen," but
obviously poor Dick was too skinny to hold down the job.
So I hired him. And he has become an invaluable asset to
our show, and just as good-looking today as he was then.

And here's our Barney Liddell a few years back, the way
he looked before he started putting on weight! He's such
a handsome boy you can't blame me for trying to whittle
him down a little, can you? Barney has got to be one of
the best-hearted men I've ever met in my life, and is a
wonderful friend to all of us in the band.

Here's Gail handing a sterling silver hoe to Myron on the occasion of his twenty-fifth anniversary with us. You might know a farmer like me would think of a gift like this. We'd heard Myron was putting in a new garden, so what could be more appropriate? (There's one very unusual thing about this picture. Myron usually cries at any kind of sentimental occasion, but here he's laughing out loud.)   *Leo North*

George Thow is just as quiet and dignified as he looks here. What you can't see are his wonderful talents and his great sense of humor.

Ken Delo, our gifted Jack-of-all-trades, is operating a hand puppet to the delight of his two children, Kimberly Anne and Kevin. Daddy looks happier than anybody! This was taken at our Christmas show. *Leo North*

Jack and Mary Lou "Singing in the Rain."   *Leo North*

Rose Weiss has been with us since the inception of our show, and her costumes—in fact, all her work—have been just perfect. Here we're celebrating a birthday together. That's Ralna at left, then Tanya, and Sandi. *Leo North*

GRAND MARSHAL—
LAWRENCE WELK
1934 PACKARD PHAETON
BRUCE MEYER

Here I am enjoying my third "term" as Grand Marshal of the Hollywood Santa Claus Lane Parade. *Mike Arnold*

This is Anne Elizabeth Martin, Queen of the Pasadena Festival of Roses Parade, at just the moment when her royal string of pearls broke and rolled all over the studio floor! As you can see, the audience always loves it when things go wrong. Look at all those laughing faces! *Tom Mareschal*

This is my very favorite junior-sized polka partner, little Michelle Semonski, who was seven and a half at the time this picture was taken. As you can see, I believe in starting them young.   *Leo North*

Believe it or not, it snows in California . . . at least it does on the road from Palm Springs to Escondido. Lu Shipstad and I couldn't resist having a snowball fight, while Lu's husband, Eddie, snapped a picture. *Eddie Shipstad*

When you take a close look at my Musical Children, I think you can see why I'm proud of them. *Tom Mareschal*

This is where it all began. Our parish church, SS Peter and Paul Roman Catholic Church in Strasburg, North Dakota.

Look what we've done! We've taken people of all races, all religions, all kinds of backgrounds—bound together only by the common notion of freedom and individual enterprise—and we've made that ideal work! We've been torn apart by the bitterest kind of dissension and suspicion between black and white, but we're in the process of making that work, too. We've established a standard of living which other nations try constantly to imitate . . . even though, at the same time, they criticize us for being too preoccupied with material gains. But I don't think we are. We continue to feed and clothe a large percentage of the hungry and homeless in the world as well as trying to solve our own problems. In our two hundred years as a family, we've survived Civil War, depression, corruption, and attacks on our Constitution . . . and for the most part, our record of achievement has been the brightest in the world.

But at this very moment, we're at the point of no return. We either climb on up to the top of the mountain—or we fall backward. We either go on to freedom and lives of fulfillment—or we fall into the waiting hands of some power structure, ready to take over our lives.

That's not just gloomy supposition on my part, either, because that same cycle has taken place in every documented civilization in history. First, you'll find a government which is a dictatorship of one kind or another; then a revolt by the people, determined to find a better life for themselves; then a strong, healthy, and growing society; then a period of moral decadence and apathy; and then finally—dictatorship again. We've followed much the same path . . . with one important difference —we've kept our freedom and hope longer than anybody else. And right now we have the greatest chance since time began to change the course of history, by putting our common sense to work and getting back to the values that built this beautiful nation—the belief in the nobility of work, of living within our means, of following the basic moral tenets which have, historically, been an integral part of our national character.

My Musical Family and I go on tour a good deal which gives me an opportunity to talk to hundreds of people. I feel close to our fans, believe in them, trust them; I value their judgment, and know they are the salt of the earth. And more and more in the past few years, as I talk to them, I've detected a sense of sadness and hopelessness on their part . . . a feeling that we're right down to the wire, and if we don't take steps to halt the direction in which we're going, it will be too late. These aren't alarmists I've been talking to. They're farmers, businessmen, entertainment personalities, mothers and fathers, and educators in every part of the country. They all agree that we are currently swamped by a wave of decadence and growing indifference.

And I wonder . . . where did it all start? Was it too much affluence? Taking the good things of life for granted? Ignoring God, and trying to change His moral laws to fit our own desires? Probably all of these, but I myself feel we made our worst mistake when we kicked God out of our schools, out of our lives . . . our hearts. When we did that we changed the moral tone of a whole nation, and today, it is a matter of deep concern. Every day on the radio or television or in the press . . . in all of our media . . . we are assailed and assaulted by false prophets, setting up false gods for us to worship, belittling the family and our religious beliefs, undermining our moral standards by glorifying what used to be considered wrong, and calling it right. I weep for the youngsters who are confronted with such an upside-down world.

If these new standards were making anybody happier, or our country better, they might have some merit. But they're not. Our divorce rate, our disease rate, our suicide and crime rates have all gone straight up. It's a crooked world when we try to live without God, and I'm convinced that the one thing that can save us is a return to God's laws.

And I have hopes that we can do so, because there are still an awful lot of fine and decent people in this country who are deeply concerned by the decaying of our moral fiber . . . the growing tendency to want something for nothing . . . or allow the strongest, or loudest, among us to take over our leadership.

It's this prospect that frightens me so, because I love our country so much. I saw first-hand how it gave life and freedom and dignity to immigrants who came here with nothing but hope. I saw what it did for my own parents. And look what it's done for me! How could I not feel grateful to a country and a free-enterprise system that let me accomplish so many of my dreams . . . and let so many millions of others accomplish theirs, too?

Whenever I feel truly downcast, I look at our orchestra . . . and my spirits shoot right up again, because to me, our band is somewhat of a little "America," too, a little democracy all its own. And if a German bandleader and a Jewish musical director can become such pals, that's a very positive sign! We are Gentile and Jew in our band, and Catholic and Protestant, and black and white, old and young, Republican and Democrat. We have backgrounds as widely divergent as those in our nation, but we're alike in our devotion to what's best for all of us. Even though we may pray to God in different churches and with different prayers, I think it's safe to say that most of us do pray.

ANOTHER DREAM

And I'm praying right now that all America will start praying again for the rebirth of the ideals our forefathers gave this country. I cannot think of a better birthday gift to give our country.

PART FOUR

THE PLAN

15

THE PLAN

I JUST COULDN'T PUT it off any longer. I had to get a clear and concise explanation of our Training and Sharing System written for the book. I'd tried several times during the year but it was never exactly what I wanted, and here we were approaching our deadline, and still no outline. I knew what the problem was. I was just so sold on our System . . . and knew from our years and years of experience how very powerful it was . . . that once I got started writing about it, I took off in all directions at once, trying to cover all its good points. I felt a little like the father who tries to tell you about his family. He usually loves them so much and is so proud of them, he doesn't quite know where to start—or when to stop!

That was my problem, too, but I kept at it. What I was after was a clear and simple account of our System, written in straightforward language, simple enough and clear enough so that anyone who wanted to try our Plan would have a reasonable idea of how it actually worked. That didn't seem so difficult until I actually tried it; and I wrote and discarded several versions till the night Bernice said, "Lawrence, what would you say is the single most important point in your Plan, the main goal—the one above all others, the ultimate objective?"

I thought for a while, and then I told her. When I'd finished, she said quietly, "That's the best explanation you've ever given. Why don't you write it just like that . . . exactly the way you told it to me?"

So I did. And if you, my good friends and readers, had been with me in my music room that night just chatting with me; and if you had asked me to explain to you, as clearly and simply as I could, just what our System is and why it means so much to me . . . this is what I would have said to you:

I

Those of you who are close and devoted fans of our programs have already seen for yourselves how our Training and Development Plan works. You've watched us over the years, and seen us grow from a small orchestra to a big Musical Family of more than fifty people. In some cases, you've watched our youngsters join us and develop into stardom almost in front of your very eyes. So perhaps I don't really need to point out the ways in which our System has helped each one of us. But I would like to tell you how it can help other people—other businessmen, in particular—and, most of all, how it can help our young people.

The primary purpose of our System is to develop people—to build humanity. When this is ac-

*complished, everything else falls into place. The
problems that face us as individuals, and as a nation, are then solved, or dramatically alleviated. So
our primary focus is and always has been to develop the people in our care to the highest degree of
their inborn talents.*

To do this, we use a method, a formula, which seeks
out and develops the best qualities within us. In actual
practice, it's a System in which an employer personally
trains and develops his people by helping them reach
their highest potential. In so doing, he releases a flood
of creative energy and good will, which is beneficial to
the entire organization. And this is done, in large part,
through the concept of sharing—and caring.

Our sharing takes several forms: Financial, emo-
tional, educational, moral, and social. The sum total
has a powerful growth-producing effect on all the people
involved—those who share as well as those who receive.

We have found over the years that this System tends
to produce superior people. So, in my opinion, it fol-
lows quite naturally that if more and more businessmen
would use it, we could produce more and more people
who are superior. This, in turn, would favorably affect
our nation, because a nation *is* its people. So most of
the trouble spots which currently plague us would to
a large extent simply disappear. Most of our social
ills . . . the moral breakdowns exemplified by wide-
spread drug usage, sexual permissiveness, violent crime,
and staggering welfare costs . . . all of these concerns
would be enormously relieved. Our financial picture
would improve because of the increased number of
healthy and successful small businesses. Our young people would have a much, much better chance to develop

themselves and their talents. And I truly believe a renewed spirit of vigor and independence would take hold of us again—a renewed belief in the honor and potentiality of our American free-enterprise system. And I cannot think of a better time than our Bicentennial Year to become again the proud and vigorous Americans we used to be . . . and are still capable of becoming.

Now how, you may be asking yourself, could one simple system accomplish all those wonderful goals? Because of the tremendous motivation involved. Our System is capable of motivating people into reaching the very top of their creative and moral endowments. And it does so by offering personal recognition and financial rewards in a warm and close manner very similar to that of a family. That is the essence of our Plan, the quality that distinguishes it and makes it so different and so effective.

One of the most important aspects of our Plan is sharing. I might say to any interested businessman . . . don't let the idea of sharing scare you. You really don't dig down into your bank account and hand out extra money. You simply share the extra profits which result from the hard work and talents of those who help you earn them. In my opinion, that is just plain good sense as well as moral justice.

In our case, we do this by sharing profits each year, as well as many other benefits. Our profit-sharing fund (maintained completely by management) is set aside and invested solely for the use of our employees. They contribute no money whatsoever in order to share in this fund. The only investment required is their goodwill, their talent, and their complete dedication.

Our other benefits are shared on the basis of merit.

Whenever one of our people does an outstanding job, we recognize it with a gift, a bonus, or a more responsible job. It could be any one of a hundred things, but whatever it is, it's designed for that person alone, something which recognizes his unique contribution to our organization. In our experience, this is far, far superior to any kind of across-the-board standard pay raises. It rewards excellence for the sake of excellence and thus motivates future excellence!

I might add also that this policy cuts across the current tendency in the world to do everything by push-button or computers which only tends to dehumanize people. We do just the opposite. We emphasize our human need for each other and recognize our people as real people, instead of just numbers on a list.

Sharing is vital to our System for four reasons:

First: Sharing motivates to the highest possible degree.

Second: It builds better business. (Each member is motivated to work better, which automatically produces a better product.)

Third: It builds character . . . the very act of sharing brings out the best in a person.

Fourth: Sharing creates happiness. This may seem like a strange by-product to list as a benefit of business-sharing, but I would say happiness in life is a goal for nearly everyone. Sharing makes people feel valued, appreciated, and respected for their abilities. Sharing gives the recognition we all should and must have for a happy life.

The most important aspect of our sharing, however, is our family spiritual sharing—something so important I will discuss it fully later on.

But sharing, as you can see from this brief outline, is essential to the successful operation of our System.

II

Second in importance to the concept of sharing is our concept of teaching . . . the manner in which we train our people and teach them the skills most useful and helpful to them in their future careers.

I believe we use the finest system of instruction available. We teach on the job; and we use our own executives as instructors—professionals who, themselves, are the best possible examples of what we're trying to teach.

We use five basic precepts in our teaching policies. We try to find our newcomers, our trainees, when they are as young as possible. There are many reasons for this, but the most important one is that we all learn better when we're young . . . and let us not forget that! Therefore, we begin training our newcomers right on the job and as young as possible. (This same idea can be translated into any other business—whether it's the food business, the dress business, the garage business, or any other kind—the principle is still the same. It's just better to learn through actual experience when you're young.)

The training is done by our production staff under my guidance. Translated into some other business, this would mean that the employer or the senior employees would do the training. Later, as the newcomer assumes his place in the organization, he in turn would train other newcomers, so the chain of responsibility is handed down. This helps build the closeness and warmth necessary for the success of our Family Sharing and Training System.

132

We pay all our trainees a salary during their training period so they earn as they learn.

The training period lasts for one year. By that time, both the employer and employee know whether the relationship is a good one and should continue. If both agree, the newcomer becomes a permanent member of the family and begins to share in the profit-sharing program.

An important by-product of our vocational training program is character development. When you work closely with someone, helping him to learn all the attributes that go into doing a good job, you invariably teach him the qualities that produce a strong character, too. (And it often works both ways. The teacher gains as well as the pupil.)

But if sharing and teaching are the building blocks of our program, freedom is the cornerstone. Without freedom our System could not function properly.

We're great believers in freedom. That's why we have no contracts in our organization. We stay together simply because we *want* to stay together, and we know in order to do so, we have to do the best possible job for each other. This means that I always try to do my best to treat my people righteously, fairly, and with their best interests at heart in every way. I'm aware that if I don't, they can walk out of my life at any time! By the same token, they make every effort to work hard, not only because they want to keep their jobs, but also because they don't want to let me or anyone else in the family down. It's the very same principle you find in a real family. Parents don't sign a contract to do certain things for their children. They do them because they love their children and want only the best for them. Children respond because they want to please their parents.

It's the same with us. In our Musical Family, I am the father, my right-hand people are the older brothers and sisters, and the younger ones are our children. And, like parents, we do for them whatever will help them fulfill their lives and become the very best persons they're capable of becoming. We do so simply because we care for them; because they are part of our family.

So, in capsule form, our System is based on:

Sharing . . . *to motivate to the highest possible degree.*
Training . . . *to build character as well as skills.*
Freedom . . . *to develop the greatest percentage of our inborn talents and reach the very top of our potential.*
And no contracts . . . *to ensure the voluntary nature of our association and underline the mutual trust and confidence we have in each other.*

Each one of these points is essential to the successful expression of our System. But perhaps one of the least understood and most important is our policy of "no contracts." Maybe I should elaborate on this point a little more fully.

III

We don't use any contracts in our System because we've found they are simply not necessary. Of course, contracts are a vital necessity in some cases—in big business for example, or large corporations, or constructing buildings, that sort of thing. But for a small business, such as ours, they are just not needed. Working without contracts seems to breed an unusual trust and closeness within an organization, a real warmth.

I treasure the close relationship I have with our kids. I would never want to feel that any of our people were afraid of me or wouldn't come to me with their fears or worries, their hopes and dreams, their jokes! I'm happy that they feel completely free to do so, and I think this free interchange of ideas is responsible for much of our progress. If there is one underlying reason for our success, it's because we have fifty people working together in mutual love and trust toward the same goal . . . fifty talents helping us create . . . fifty minds thinking in our behalf. So when I siphon off the best of our suggestions and ideas, I am choosing from among fifty men and women all working toward the same thing, and that makes us fifty times as powerful as we'd be otherwise. So believe me! . . . I want to keep those lines of communication open at all times.

Our policy of No Contracts helps assure this. A contract can be something of a wall between people, and if you do run into trouble spots of any kind, then you have to deal with a lawyer or some other party, and immediately you lose the personal one-to-one relationship so vital to the success of our System. I have learned to know our people so well through our System that in most cases I fully understand their frustrations or personality problems, and it makes it far easier for me to help them, far easier to work out our problems together.

But a contract tends to separate you . . . almost pits you against each other. And there is no contract in the world which could possibly cover every eventuality anyway. We prefer to rely on our policy of no contracts, which guarantees that the only way to stay together is to treat each other the best we can . . . the Golden Rule in action.

This means, also, that our System is self-regulating. It would not be possible for an employer using our Plan to take advantage of his people in any way. If he did, they just wouldn't stay with him. And it works both ways. In our Musical Family, I've found that if one of our kids fails to do his share, I rarely have to get involved or even mention it. The others, in the time-honored tradition of brothers and sisters everywhere, do it for me and let the offender know pretty quickly that he's not pulling his weight. And in most cases that's all it takes!

I would say that our System works so effectively because each one of its main points supports the others. Our financial sharing offers tremendous motivation. Our teaching program sharpens our skills and helps us explore and develop our expanding potential. Our policy of no contracts builds mutual respect and trust. And all of these factors combine to provide the most powerful element of all . . . something as difficult to define—and as powerful—as love itself; in fact, it *is* a form of love, and it is the unquestioned source of our strength.

IV

The heart of our Plan is "heart." That's the best way I can explain it. I see it over and over again in my own relationships with the kids and in their relationships with each other. The girls, particularly, are very close—forever giving each other showers, parties, and celebrations, helping each other rehearse, exchanging recipes, acting like sisters. And when one of them is expecting a baby, everything goes into high gear! We all get involved then, making sure our expectant mama doesn't have to work too hard, or stand around too long. And we go to great lengths trying to hide her condition from the camera. Of course, we've been doing that ever since the Lennons were with us. There was a time when it seemed to me that all the lovely Lennons were having babies one right after another. I guess maybe I'm exaggerating, but I do recall Rose and the wardrobe girls going slightly mad trying to think up new ways to camouflage them.

Then, after the Lennons left, Tanya and Sandi put our ingenuity to the test on four separate occasions—Tanya with Lawrence Welk the Third and Kevin, and Sandi with her little Ami and Jenni. One day during the writing of this book, Sandi came to my dressing room, smiling, a very special gleam in her eyes. She just stood there for a moment, beaming, and then said, "Guess what?" I took one look at that happy face, and I said, "Well, I don't think I have to guess very hard, Sandi. You're going to have a new little baby, aren't you?" "Yes, I am," she said joyfully, "and Brent and I are so excited." We were all pleased for Sandi—she's such a great favorite.

So for the next few months, Rose racked her brain to come up with gowns which would conceal Sandi's expanding figure and still look good on Mary Lou and Gail; and Jim and Jack worked out ways to stage the girls' number. They had Sandi standing behind the piano or a couch, peeking between the fronds of a palm tree, or peering around the side of Richard Maloof's big bass tuba—anything big enough to hide her and still show her happy, glowing face. We had a lot of fun

137

planning these deceptions, and I teased Sandi about it. "Now, Sandi," I said, "since we're going to all this trouble for you, the least you can do is call the baby Lawrence, if it's a boy."

The baby was not expected till the end of January, but on January 13, 1976, just after I arrived at the studio to begin taping for the day, Lois stuck her head in my dressing room door and said, "Sandi's husband is on the phone." Somehow I knew immediately just what had happened, so I picked up the phone and said, "Boy or girl?" "Uh . . . uh . . . uh, boy!" shouted Brent, startled that I'd guessed and overjoyed that he and Sandi had a son. We chatted for a few minutes, exchanging congratulations and vital statistics . . . "eight pounds, four ounces, born at three o'clock this morning" . . . and then I said, "Brent, that's wonderful. And you're calling him Lawrence. Now isn't that nice!" There was a slight pause and then Brent said, "Uh, well, no, as a matter of fact, we're calling him Benjamin Brent after the man who married us. He's a very good friend of ours." "Well," I said, trying my best to sound insulted, "I thought *I* was a very good friend of yours, too!" We kidded some more and I asked Brent to give Sandi our love and best wishes, and then I raced around the studio telling everybody the big news. Cheers and hurrahs erupted all over the place with much excitement.

Sandi had been scheduled to sing in the trio that day, so I thought I'd try a little experiment and see if Diane, the oldest Semonski girl, could sing Sandi's part, and she worked hard all day learning the song. That night she did very well in the trio, which made me very happy, and the three girls sang the song as a tribute to Sandi's firstborn son, Benjamin Brent Griffiths. It was almost as if we were welcoming a new nephew, a new grandson, into our family. That's one kind of "heart" I mean.

The girls had earlier given Sandi a shower, as they always do for each other. (They even gave Norma a shower when her son Ron and his wife, Candi, were expecting their first child!) "Well, she's done so much for all of us," said Tanya at the time, "we'd like to do something for her." Cissy sometimes kiddingly complains about going to so many showers. "Just wait," the other girls tell her. "If you ever decide to get married, we'll give you a shower that'll last for a week."

There are frequent get-togethers, and Fern and I have a big Christmas party every year and everybody comes—the band and all their families, the office staff and all theirs, and our own personal friends. Our people babysit for each other, go on trips together, and help each other in time of trouble. When the earthquake hit us in 1971, for example, and Don Staples' and Neil Levang's homes were badly damaged, several of the fellows immediately offered the use of their homes till the crisis was over.

I think maybe that is when our "heart" shows up most of all—during the tough times, the heartbreaking times. When Lois was sick, all of us were so worried. I went to the hospital to see her nearly every morning on my way to work. I'd talk to her quietly for a few moments and she'd answer me quite coherently, and I thought maybe I was helping keep her spirits up. (After she recovered, though, she told me she didn't remember a thing about it, so I guess I could have saved my breath.) But, naturally, I was concerned about her— we all were. Sam and Don made sure she had the best doctors and best care. Everybody in the band called the hospital or visited, sent cards and letters, and said prayers. We all knew that there was a chance Lois might not live through the surgery, or that she could be impaired even if she did. But thanks to the Good Lord, she came through beautifully and within three months was back at work with us again. The love that was operating in her behalf was very powerful then.

There was the time Jim Roberts was so sick years ago, before I even realized we had a System. We were still playing at the Aragon Ballroom in Santa Monica when I noticed Jim was sitting down an awful lot, and lying down an awful lot. At first I was annoyed. I thought he was falling down on the job, literally! But it soon developed he was a very sick boy. The worst of it was that the doctors couldn't seem to diagnose his trouble. Jim kept going, insisting he was well enough to perform. I didn't want to break his spirit, so I went along with him. The other boys drove him to and from the ballroom and he rested between each number. But still the weight melted off him and he just faded away right before our eyes. One night he collapsed completely and was rushed off to the hospital. There, one of the doctors discovered at the last moment that he was suffering from Addison's disease, and administered lifesaving antidotes. From then on it was just a matter of maintaining the proper medication, and today Jim is absolutely fine. But he has often told us how helpful and encouraging it was to him to know how much we cared during those dark, dark days.

But in some ways I think the story of Larry Hooper explains better than anything else what I'm trying to say.

When Larry fell ill a few years ago and needed open-heart surgery, our whole family responded instantly. All the boys either telephoned or went directly down to the hospital to give blood. The girls called Beverly Hooper, Larry's wife, and offered to babysit so she could stay at the hospital with him. We assured Larry he had nothing to worry about, that his place in the family was there waiting. And that instantaneous, wholehearted response was such a comfort to Larry. When I went down to the hospital to see him—and found him lying helplessly in a tangle of tubes and bottles and glasses, he was still able to look up at me with that wonderful, warm, unmistakable Hooper smile.

He was a terribly sick man, dreadfully ill for a long, long, time. After the initial surgery he developed one complication after another, and on two different occasions he was given up completely. But both times he rallied and fought hard to live. I'll never forget the day Sam Lutz and I went down to see him. Larry is a big man, about six feet tall, and normally weighs around one hundred and eighty pounds. But this day, when the orderlies brought him into the room and laid him quietly on his bed, it was painful, really painful to look at him. He weighed only ninety-one pounds and was literally skin and bones. But even then he had a twinkle in his eyes and a ghost of a smile on his face. His wife told us later that the constant phone calls and letters and cards from the kids were helping him more than we could ever know.

He had an unbelievably slow convalescence, and at one point lost the use of his voice completely—that marvelous deep bass voice of his. We all felt so bad about that. But, miraculously, after another year his voice came back, and little by little, day by day, he seemed to improve.

The girls continued to babysit and give Beverly a few hours off now and then. The fellows went out to the house and did the heavy work Larry could no longer do. Dick Dale was especially close to the family and helped in so many different ways. We stayed close, trying to let him know we were with him every step of the way. We never forgot our cards and letters and phone calls.

One day, four years after Larry was stricken, I was sitting quietly in my dressing room at the studio when I became aware of someone standing in the doorway. I looked up and there was Larry—tall, strong, his weight fully recovered, the same wonderful smile on his face, the same warm twinkle in his eyes. He stood gazing at me for a moment, and then his eyes filled with tears and he said, simply, "Well, Boss . . . I'm home." I couldn't speak. And my own eyes filled with tears as I threw my arms around this man who had been such a close part of our lives for so many years. Then the whole room was full of people . . . the girls came flying in, tears streaming down their faces, flinging their arms around Larry, hugging him, kissing him, welcoming him home; the fellows doing the same thing, shaking his hand, thumping him on the back. The rehearsal came to an absolute standstill while everyone clustered around Larry to let him know how much we loved him, how happy we were that all our hopes and dreams for him had come true.

After the first big excitement, I took him out onstage and introduced him to the studio audience. Most of them had known about his long, long struggle to live, and when they saw him standing there in the center of the stage—tall, strong, beaming happily, almost shyly— they rose to their feet and gave him a standing ovation. The boys in the band stood up, too, as they applauded. I stood at the side of the stage, my baton tucked underneath my arm, joining in the thunderous applause, happy in the way only those of us who have nearly lost someone very dear to us can understand. Beside me Beverly Hooper was applauding fiercely, too; her own eyes wet with tears as she watched her husband

stand onstage, back where he belonged after an almost
unbelievably long struggle. Then she turned to me,
touched me lightly on the arm and said very softly,
"Lawrence, how can I ever thank you? You . . . you
saved his life."

I didn't save his life. The "family" did. His wonderful wife, his children, and devoted doctors deserve
most of the credit, of course. But in Larry's own words,
the knowledge that we were there waiting for him,
praying for him, caring for him while he was away,
was a powerful stimulus to his recovery. And I think
it says better than any words of mine, the kind of sharing, the kind of "heart" I mean.

This love, this sharing of self is the powerful energy
that makes everything else in our System function so
well. And I honestly believe the same mysterious and
wonderful sense of caring would arise in any other
organization that tried our System, because I know
from experience how sharing tends to stimulate a warm
and growing affection for each other. And also, I really
cannot imagine any businessman being interested in
trying our System in the first place unless he truly liked
people and was a fairly warm and compassionate man
himself . . . and, most certainly, a man who was motivated by far more than just a desire to make money!

Because our System won't work if all you want is to
make money. But if you want to make your life happier and you'd like to help others, then this System
could be perfect for you. And the chances are, your
business will improve anyway. All my life I've concentrated on the goal, on people, on the job at hand,
and I can honestly and truly say I've never thought
about money. But I've discovered that when you put
everything you have into reaching your goal, then the
money seems to come along anyway.

THE PLAN

So when people ask me what kind of man is best suited to install this System in his organization, I say: Anyone who knows his business thoroughly and is willing to take the time and trouble of teaching it; anyone who likes people and who lives his life, or at least tries to live it, according to God's Laws. It doesn't take someone of superior intellect, vast wealth, or enormous power. It just takes someone who cares.

So that is our Plan—a System of sharing and training in an atmosphere of total freedom, unhindered by contracts; of helping each other develop our highest, best qualities . . . and then trusting in each other to live up to them; in short . . . of developing our own human nature to the highest possible degree.

In essence, our System is really an adaptation of the free-enterprise system as it was originally meant to be. Our founding fathers believed that each one of us should have the right and the freedom to live up to his greatest capabilities, without any roadblocks or barriers being thrown in his path, as long as he didn't infringe on the rights of anyone else.

That's exactly what we believe. That's exactly what we're trying to do. And I have hopes that through our Family System we may be able to bring back the true meaning of free enterprise once again—and save it for generations to come.

16

THE SQUARE—ME!

THERE'S MORE TO WRITING a book than just writing a book. You have to come up with pictures, a foreword, a dedication, explanatory illustrations, and . . . a title. I always have a lot of ideas for titles . . . although I have to admit I was on the losing end with my suggestions for my first two books. Nevertheless, I was very pleased with the final choices. *Wunnerful, Wunnerful!* seemed just right for the title of my life story, and *Ah-One, Ah-Two!* a natural for my second book. But as we neared the deadline for our third, we still hadn't settled on a title, and every day I came up with new ideas—or my friends did. (I might say to any of you folks who are planning on writing a book—don't ask your friends for suggestions. They'll tell you—and you'll end up more confused than ever!) But one day I had such a sensational idea I knew I had found the absolutely perfect title, and I just couldn't wait till Bernice came over that night to tell her. The minute she walked in the door I said, "Guess what! I have the perfect title. It's absolutely sensational!" "Really?" she said, dumping her tape recorder, notebooks, and papers all over the coffee table. "Tell me quick . . . what is it?"

"Well," I said, barely able to restrain my enthusiasm and beaming from ear to ear, "this is it! Are you ready? Hold your breath now!" I threw my arms wide and said, dramatically, *"The Square!"*

Bernice used to be an actress, so after a split second she assumed a terrifically interested expression. "Mmmmm!" she said. "Well, my goodness . . . now that's really something! Let me just think about that for a few days." Then her face brightened and she said, "Or I'll tell you—let me ask Dennis Fawcett at Prentice-Hall. He's had *so* much more experience with titles than I have!"

Well, you don't have to hit me over the head to make a point, and I could see she was not exactly enthusiastic about it. But I liked it . . . liked the idea behind it and what it stood for. Years before, I had come across a famous speech by Charles H. Brower called "The Return of the Square," and I liked it so much I had Aladdin, who used to recite poetry on our show, read it for the television audience. I still have several pamphlets with copies of that speech in my files. But actually, the idea of using *The Square* for a title had occurred to me just a few days earlier while Fern and I were spending a week at our vacation home in Indian Wells near Palm Springs with our good friends Eddie and Lu Shipstad. Eddie and I had played golf every day, and Fern and Lu had shopped to their hearts' content. Fern had discovered a restaurant called Young's Cafeteria, which served the kind of home-cooked food we all liked, and we'd eaten several of our meals there. One night as we were driving back to the house, Fern was enthusiastically telling all of us some

146

story, and she happened to mention the word "square." A few minutes later she did it again; and then a third time. Finally, I said, "Honey, please, you know how sensitive I am. Do you have to use that word so often? That . . . that bothers me!"

We all laughed because we all know I'm not the least bit sensitive about it. In fact, in this day and age I'm kind of proud of being called a square! That label had been applied to me by many critics during my earliest days with the band, especially on television. It may be some indication of just how square I used to be when I tell you folks I really wasn't sure what the term meant—although I had a pretty good idea! I even went so far as to look it up in the dictionary, but that wasn't much help. The first definition said "square" meant a four-sided, box-like shape; the next said it was an instrument (that seemed a little closer to my profession) used for measuring. But neither definition was very helpful. Actually, I knew deep down in my bones what it meant anyway. To be "square" meant being "old-fashioned," "believing in traditional values," enjoying "corn" (on the cob or in music). I did all those things, so how could I quarrel with that?

Besides, when I was growing up, "square" was a compliment. You gave a man a square deal, looked him square in the eye, stood foursquare on your principles. If you didn't owe anybody a dime, you were square with the world—and what a wonderful feeling that was!

I grew up in a community of squares. I felt at home with them. And even today, I'd say that most of the fans we meet on our tours may be somewhat on the square side. I'd be willing to bet that the vast majority of them pay their bills (they may scream at the size of their tax bill but they'll pay it.) They keep their children clothed and fed, send them to Sunday school, raise them to believe in God and this country. They take their voting privileges seriously, too, because with all its faults . . . our country is still the greatest in the world, and we squares would like to keep it that way. Squares are the ones who keep their houses neat and clean, their lawns mowed, and put the flag out on the Fourth of July and other holidays. The squares of this world are the ones who keep the wheels greased so the rest of the world can have a little smoother ride.

Mentioning the word "grease" brings to mind a story which only proves to you folks how square I used to be. Years ago the boys and I were playing our first big job at the William Penn Hotel in Pittsburgh, and we were invited to make some recordings in New York. Driving home in our seven-passenger Pierce Arrow, excitedly talking about our big adventure, we were cruising along on the turnpike about thirty-five miles an hour—right along with the regular flow of traffic—when suddenly from out of the blue, a motorcycle officer zoomed up and ordered me to pull over to the side. I couldn't imagine what I'd done wrong, but the officer told me almost immediately. "What's your hurry?" he demanded, as he strolled over to the car. "You were speeding!" "Really!" I said, honestly puzzled. "I'm terribly sorry officer . . . I had no idea . . . I thought I was driving right along with everyone else." "Nope," he said, getting out his book. "You were going a little over the speed limit. I'm afraid I'll have to give you a ticket." At this, there were squawks of outrage from the other boys but I shushed them quickly —I didn't want to make things worse than they were. And again I told the officer that I'd had no idea I was driving over the limit, and again he said he was very sorry but he was afraid he'd have to give me a ticket. This conversation went on and on with him repeating over and over that he was afraid he'd be forced to give me a ticket, and me on pins and needles waiting. Suddenly then, after close to half an hour, he slammed his book shut, growled, "Well, I'll let you go this time, but watch your speed!" jumped back on his motorcycle, and zoomed off! I couldn't figure the whole thing out and when I got home to Pittsburgh I told my good close friend Allan Baylor about it. "'Why do you suppose he kept me there for such a long time and then didn't give me a ticket after all?" I asked him innocently. Allan looked at me pityingly. "Oh you dummy," he said, shaking his head. "Don't you know you were supposed to 'grease the palms of his hands'?" I paused . . . a little shook . . . as this information sunk in. To a farmer like me, "grease" meant only one thing—the thick heavy black axle grease we used on the farm machinery back home. "Really?" I said, mystified. "But Allan, why would anyone want me to put grease on the palms of their hands?" (I told you I was a square!)

While all of us squares may not be quite so naive as that and I can't claim positively that the great majority of us don't swear or tell off-color jokes, I have to admit that this is one square who can't do either one. I just never learned how. The worst I can come up with, even when I miss an easy putt on the golf course, is "Oh, shucks!" (My friends tell me this sounds worse anyway.) Most of the squares I know would rather laugh at a good clean joke any day than one a little on the blue side. (I'm not trying to set myself up as a paragon, by the way. I have my share of faults, as the boys in the band are only too happy to tell me. But I keep trying to overcome them, with a certain amount of success. And I've discovered that the older I get, the easier it becomes!)

Squares as a group tend to enjoy clean fun, understandable music, pretty and wholesome girls, and entertainment that builds up and doesn't tear down. I've staked my whole career on that and, of course, in show business you're laying your career on the line every single show. It doesn't matter what your rating was last week, it has to stay up there, and you have to come up with a program that's entertaining enough so the folks won't say, "Let's see what's on the other channels!" or, "I think I'll just get myself a beer." I don't want to give anybody a chance to do anything like that. We all work hard to keep our show bright and entertaining—something the whole family will enjoy.

Maybe that's why I don't object to the word "square" —because it's tied in so closely with the family. One of the things Charles H. Brower said in his famous "The Return of the Square" was "A square is a slob who gets all choked up when the band plays 'America the Beautiful' . . . a man who dearly loves his family and his country—and is honestly sentimental about both."

Well, I kind of feel that way myself. So when reporters ask me, as they do to this day, "Mr. Welk, how does it make you feel when people call you a 'square'?" I tell them exactly how it feels. It feels just fine.

There's a postscript to this little story. A couple of weeks after Bernice relayed my suggestion to Dennis Fawcett, he called to say they had found a title they liked a little better. "We've just read your manuscript," he said, "and we think we have the perfect title. It's *My America, Your America*. What do you think of that, Mr. Welk?"

"I love it," I told him. And I do.

17

CHRISTMAS IN NOVEMBER

As 1975 DREW TO a close, a great many nice things happened, and again I marvelled that my life should be so wonderful, so filled with happiness. One of the happier surprises was my invitation to be the grand marshal of the Hollywood Santa Claus Parade, a festive evening parade, traditional in Hollywood for the past forty-four years. I got a call the Friday evening before the event from a frantic committee who had just learned that Bob Hope, originally scheduled to be the marshal, had a sudden change of plans which prevented his appearance. "Won't you please help us out?" they pleaded. They went on in such a rush of explanations, I realized they were afraid my feelings would be hurt because they hadn't asked me first! So I said, "Well, now, let me look at my appointment book and see. Yes, I have that evening free. I'll be happy to do it for you. And don't worry," I added, "I'm used to playing second fiddle!"

But as the night of the parade approached, I began to have second thoughts because we had a sudden

unusual cold spell—cold, that is, for Hollywood—and
the temperature plummeted downward. I played golf
with Eddie Shipstad very early on two of those morn-
ings and I wore a fur hat with ear flaps, extra socks,
and so many sweaters I could hardly swing. So the
thought of riding in an open car in the parade in the cold
night air for an hour or so was not exactly thrilling.
Still, I had grown up in North Dakota where below-
freezing weather was common, and I figured my blood
couldn't have thinned that much over the years.

But on the night of the parade I decided to take no
chances. I dressed as warmly as possible in my heaviest
suit and thickest long woolen golf socks, and if I'd
owned a suit of long underwear I'd have worn that,
too. But I didn't, so I took along a couple of extra
coats and a blanket, just in case. I didn't need them
though. When I arrived I found I was to ride in the
back seat of the most luxurious Packard I had ever seen.
It was huge, pale green, and open, with no roof at all.
But it was also heated and had a heavy glass partition
between the front and back seats so I was warm as
toast and didn't need my blanket or coats. I don't think
I would have needed them anyway, the crowd was so
warm and friendly. I always get a kick out of watching
how people wave along a parade route—the really little
ones, the babies, just wiggle their fingers; the older children wave both arms frantically; and I can usually
spot our fans, because they wave an imaginary baton,
pop an imaginary champagne cork, or dance a couple
of steps. I waved, smiled, and popped a few imaginary
corks myself and thoroughly enjoyed it. I'd been Hollywood Parade marshal a couple of times before (one
year I took Bobby and Cissy along with me), and I'd
also been honored as the grand marshal of the great
Tournament of Roses Parade in Pasadena in 1972.

In fact, another nice thing that happened during those waning days of November was having the current queen of the Rose Parade and her court appear on our show. Everything went off well till the lovely young queen and I danced the polka, when suddenly her royal string of pearls broke and rolled every which way. That was the end of any formality for the evening! The queen reverted instantly to a seventeen-year-old schoolgirl with an acute case of the giggles, and we all broke up laughing.

But the nicest thing of all was the afternoon the Semonskis came to my dressing room a week before our Christmas show and asked to speak to me. "Certainly, girls," I said, as they all filed in with their parents. "What can I do for you?"

Instead of answering, they grouped themselves quickly into a semicircle, and as their father touched a chord on his accordion, broke into a song. I was charmed. It was a new song and they were singing it well. But best of all they'd done it all on their own. The minute they finished, I started to congratulate them but, with beaming faces, they launched into another brand new song. And before I could say anything they sang a third! I was just delighted. To think they'd done this all on their own, said more to me than anything else. I asked two of the girls to sing the lead in one of the songs while the rest of them harmonized in the background. They followed my directions so perfectly I felt a surge of real satisfaction, and an even stronger surge of gratitude to Bob Ballard, George Cates, Curt Ramsey, Jim Hobson, Jack Imel, and all the rest of our staff—especially Gail Farrell. All of them had given so freely of their skill, time, and care and worked with such dedication that the girls were singing better than any of us could have expected. Not only were they singing with more professionalism, they were singing with the excitement, the inner assurance which comes from doing something entirely on your own. And I knew—finally and completely—the time had come to tell them what I'd wanted to tell them for several weeks.

"Girls," I said, "sit down for a moment. I have something I've been wanting to say to you." They all sat down, looking slightly apprehensive. "Young ladies," I said and then paused, looking sternly at each one of them in turn, "young ladies"—(another long pause—) "I am terribly . . . terribly . . . proud of you!" They all burst into excited squeals of relief, giggling a little, eyes sparkling.

"You know, there were many times during this past year when I was really worried about you. I was afraid maybe this time I'd bitten off a little too big a chunk to chew. But you've come through just the way I'd dreamed—maybe even better than I hoped. You have really learned how to work! And so," I looked around that circle of eager, hopeful young faces, "I think you can now consider yourselves permanent members of our Musical Family." I opened my arms wide. "You are now my Musical Children."

All six girls rushed into my arms at once, crying, laughing, talking all at the same time, hugging and kissing each other and me, with little Michelle grabbing me tightly around the knees, her blue eyes blazing, the parents standing in the background, shedding a few tears, too. It was a happy moment, a very happy moment, and I felt so good about the fact that the girls had finally made it—partly, of course, because their success justified the faith I had in our Family Training System, and partly because I was just so pleased for them and their parents, who had been a constant source of support and encouragement.

When things quieted down a little I said, "Girls, I have something else I want to say. We've all helped you, that's true, but you have really done this by yourselves. Nothing can stop you now—except yourselves. If you keep your sweetness and wholesomeness and you keep on working on yourselves and your songs, I truly believe you can become one of America's favorite sister acts!" Six faces began to glow even brighter, six pairs of eyes shone with excitement as they considered this new goal. (As you can see, I never stop motivating people! I'm a firm believer that once you stand still, you start slipping backward. And I really did believe that if the girls retained the niceness, the sweetness their parents had instilled in them, they had every chance of long-lasting success.) As they filed out I hugged each of them and said, "Girls, do something for me, will you? Please stay as nice as you are, and we'll keep on helping you."

I must say that was an extremely satisfying moment for me. These little girls . . . these little schoolgirls who had had nothing much more than individually pleasant voices plus a desire to succeed . . . had turned themselves into professionals in less than a year. I looked at their parents and I knew we were thinking the same thing. All of us had had dreams of glory for the girls but the girls and their parents, too, to a certain extent had been mainly thinking of the glamor of it—the fun of just standing in front of a camera looking pretty and singing nice songs. They had had no concept at the time they began, of the work involved, the dedication, the constant striving to achieve the perfection necessary for success.

But they'd done it. They had not only learned to

sing better, they had become better young people themselves. They had learned that the only way to make something of yourself is to work at it constantly and do it yourself. I was very, very happy about that. One of the great joys of my life is to help other people develop their potential. And to think that the little Semonskis, who seemed to have so many strikes against them when they started out, had finally made it was a wonderful feeling. If I had given the girls a Christmas present a little early, they had most certainly done the same thing for me.

It was an especially happy occasion when we all gathered together a week or so later to tape our Christmas show. Christmas comes a little early in our family because we tape all our programs six weeks in advance. For weeks before that, Lois and the girls in the office arrange for dozens of presents for the children and wrap them in bright papers and ribbons to be distributed on the show. George Thow writes special material, George Cates gets out the lovely carols we sing every year, and he and Bob Ballard rehearse the kids. All of the costumes and special decorations that go into the show are brought out, dusted off, and polished up, keeping alive the traditions that have come to mean so much to all of us.

My own family makes preparations to be on the show because that's also a long-time tradition. All of us bring our younger children, which means that we have twenty or thirty children onstage under the age of thirteen . . . at least half of them under the age of six. They all turn up, dazzling in their Christmas finery, little faces scrubbed, hair combed, the girls in their prettiest party dresses.

This time Sandi Griffiths brought her two beautiful little girls, Jenni and Ami, both of whom looked like Christmas angels; Tanya brought our Buns and Kevin; Ken Delo and his lovely wife, Marilyn, had their beautiful children there; all the fellows brought their wives and kiddies; and the excitement level was very, very high.

I was trying to be everywhere at once, consoling a little one who was threatening to break into tears, listening to Joe Feeney's youngsters rehearse their number, talking to my own family—Fern, Shirley and her brood, Donna and Jim and theirs. Shirley caused a momentary bit of excitement when she failed to show up in time for the first rehearsal. I went looking for her and found her giggling in the hallway outside. "What's so funny?" I asked her. "Well," she gasped, "I just came down from the makeup room . . . and the makeup man put me in that reclining chair, and then he bent over and stared at me for the longest time. Finally he said, 'My, oh my! How long do I have to make up that face?' " Shirley went off into a gale of giggles again. Well, I don't think I'll be accused of being a proud father when I say that Shirley is really a very pretty lady. And I still think the makeup man was simply pleased that he had such a nice face to work on. But Shirley evidently didn't think so. She got into such a fit of the giggles when I asked her on camera to tell the folks what the makeup man had said that she burst out laughing again. If you saw that show and noticed her laughter . . . now you know why.

The whole show had a gaiety and happiness to it. It's hard for me to convey the feeling I get at that time. I'm surrounded by the people I love most in my life— my own family, my Musical Family, and our wonderful family of fans and friends who are there to see the show. I feel fulfilled. It makes every bit of effort I've ever extended in my life worthwhile, every bit of self-denial and self-discipline I've brought to bear on myself worth it. Those hours together, singing and cele-brating Christmas with my loved ones close to me are among my happiest hours—my real treasures.

So I cuddled my own grandchildren—little Christine who had painstakingly learned a piano solo "for Grandpa," little Lisa, and all the others. And I watched while Buns proceeded to try to lead the band. If there's one of my grandchildren who seems likely to step into Grandpa's shoes, it's this little boy, Lawrence Welk the Third! And I enjoyed it as much as the kids when Dick Dale, our resident Santa Claus, came in dressed in the famous red suit and white whiskers, dragging a sleigh loaded with presents which he proceeded to pass out to all the eager little hands.

By five-thirty we had concluded that part of the tap-ing. In the olden days we used to tape the children as part of the Christmas show at the regular time of eight o'clock, but we had such frazzled nerves and ex-hausted kiddies on our hands by that time that we learned to tape the children's segment early and do the rest of the show later. Again, a case of learning by doing!

I went downstairs to rest for a moment and have a bite to eat. I rarely have a full meal on taping days. In twenty-five years of doing television shows, I don't think I've had more than twenty-five real dinners. I much prefer to nibble on the snacks I buy at the little corner grocery store on my way to the studio. I usually load up with a sack full of canned puddings (especially tapioca), bananas, cheese, crackers (Triscuit, natural-ly), and packets of Carnation instant breakfast. All those things seem to agree with my nervous stomach.

So I munched and sipped as I waited for Rudy Horvatich to come in and touch up my makeup, which is mainly a matter of darkening my eyebrows and my hair at the temples where it's starting to get gray. Rudy, who's a master at his job, does everything swiftly and painlessly. Every time I see him, I'm reminded of the time a lady came to see our show years ago and somehow got past the guards and into the dressing room area backstage where she spotted me being ministered to by the current makeup man. She stopped in her tracks, fascinated, and came wheeling over to watch over his shoulder as he worked on my face. She never said one word till he had finished his job and whipped off my makeup cape. Then she turned to him and said with undisguised admiration, "Sir, you are a genius!" (Like father, like daughter, I guess. Shirley and I do have our moments with makeup men!)

After Rudy left, I got dressed in my Christmas clothes and went back onstage to greet the incoming studio audience for the evening performance. That's always one of my favorite parts of the show—talking with the guests who take the trouble to come to see us. Even after fifty-two years in the business, I'm always filled with wonder and gratitude at how generous our fans are . . . so kind, so interested in our show that they make every appearance a party. I chat with them, find out where they're from, maybe dance a polka or two, sometimes find a little talent in the audience to entertain us. Sometimes Myron Floren comes out with his accordion or Bob Ralston plays the organ or little Michelle Semonski sings a song by herself. But as much as I enjoy our preshow visit, my ears are always cocked for the sound of Jim Hobson's voice from the control booth upstairs, warning "five minutes," and I race back to my spot before the microphone, ready for the moment which still fills me with such excitement and joy—the sound of the band, the sound of the music filling my ears, my head, my heart. That's the time I come to life most of all.

And that particular Christmas show was especially moving for me, particularly when all our kids, dressed in their carolers' costumes, joined together in the lovely carols that always bring my youth back so sharply to me. I'll never get away from my roots and I never want to. I think it's important to remember our beginnings, our homes, the love that gave us birth. Every time I hear those Christmas carols, I am right back in our little church in Strasburg at midnight mass on Christmas Eve again . . . the church heavy with the scent of pine boughs and wreaths, the flickering candles on the altar, the manger scene—it all comes back. Listening to our kids sing "Silent Night" reminded me vividly of the way our entire congregation used to stand and sing that lovely old hymn, each family singing and celebrating Christmas together—as a family.

And that's just what my Musical Family and I were doing—celebrating Christmas together, as a family. Only this year we had extra cause to celebrate. Because this year, we had six little sisters.

PART FIVE

A LOOK
AHEAD

18

A LOOK AHEAD

WHEN WE TAPED OUR last show of the season, I felt, as always, that strange combination of relief and sadness—satisfaction that we had concluded one of our very best years, and a kind of melancholy that it was all over. We taped the last two shows on two succeeding days, always a heavy schedule. And to my vast annoyance, not to say pain, I complicated things for myself by throwing out my back! I've been bothered off and on over the years with my back which occasionally goes out on me. It happens only rarely and always in the simplest possible way—never through some big dramatic accident. This time, about six in the morning on the day of the show, I was soaping away in my shower as I've done a few thousand times before, standing on one leg like a stork while I washed the other foot, when suddenly something went *snap!* There I was, immobilized, rigid with pain, and wondering not only how I was going to get out of the shower and into my clothes, but how I was going to get through the day!

Well, I managed to get out of the shower by clutching the walls and moving very stiffly the way you do when you're afraid one false move and your head may fall off, and I finally got dressed and into my car. By that time, I'd made up my mind not to say anything to anybody. I knew if I did, they'd be so concerned they'd spend more time trying to make me comfortable than they would working on the show, and that wouldn't help any of us. So I gritted my teeth and kept my backache to myself, and I moved very, very carefully all through that first show. (And a strange thing happened. I had to lead a long concert arrangement of songs from *My Fair Lady,* and while I was doing so, the pain left me. As soon as I finished, the pain came right back. Music has the power to change my life in more ways than one, I guess.) Other than that, it was one of the most painful days I've ever experienced, and the moment I got home that night, I took some medication the doctors prescribed and fell right into bed with a heating pad tucked underneath my back.

Next morning it seemed even worse . . . and only those of you who've had bad backs know what a production it is to get out of bed in the morning. You have to sort of roll out, still on your back, and then come up, inch by painful inch, till you're more or less standing upright. But once again I managed it and again kept my mouth shut, not telling anyone at the studio, not even Jim, how I felt. That night my daughter Donna, her husband, Jim, and Bernice, too, came down to the show, since it was the closing performance. They knew about my ailment, but very few others did. Even though a few of the folks in the audience may have wondered why I didn't dance the polka, I don't think anyone really gave it a second thought.

The show that night was exceptional . . . really fine.

Jim had outdone himself with special effects. In one number he had Sandi, Gail, and Mary Lou flying in a hang-gliding machine; in another, Norma and Jim Roberts pedaled merrily down the freeway on a bike. I don't pretend to know how Jim manages these effects, and even if I did I don't think I could explain them! Anyway, it all went off flawlessly and, in spite of my pain, I was delighted. As the show drew to a close I began to feel an almost overwhelming sense of relief. I had made it, actually made it through both shows, without falling down once! I was standing in the middle of the stage congratulating myself as the orchestra began playing our closing theme, when suddenly from out of nowhere Ralna hurled herself at me and began dragging me toward a microphone on the far side of the stage. "Oh, no, no, no!" I gasped, trying to fend her off, as she kept pulling my arm. "No, oh, Ralna, please!" She stopped, startled, realizing something was wrong, and said quickly, "But Jim wants you to move in front of this mike," and we managed to stumble over in time for my closing announcement. While I may never get an Academy Award for acting, I think I should at least get honorable mention—what a performance I put on! I smiled, waved, read our closing lines, and all the time I was petrified for fear I'd fall down, topple over, or faint dead away. The moment we went off the air I explained to Ralna and the others what had happened, and they were so sympathetic I almost began to enjoy the whole thing. Afterward, I made my way stiffly down the stairs to my dressing room. Then I was faced with the prospect of getting out of my stage clothes and into my own shirt and slacks. That was bad enough, but when it came to bending over and putting on my shoes, I just couldn't do it. Rose finally came to my rescue. Grabbing a shoe horn and shoving me in and out of my shoes, she said, "Well, I've dressed plenty of little boys in my time, but never a big boy like you!"

Don and Sam were waiting with us because they had arranged a party for the cast and crew in the dining room of the studio. At first I didn't think I could make it, but then I realized how much I wanted to see the kids and tell them how wonderful I thought they were. And also, because I always drive Lois, Russ, and Henry Cuesta down to the studio with me, I knew if I went home they'd have to miss the party, too. So, holding on to Lois on one side and Bernice on the other, I trudged step by slow step out of the studio and a block or so to the party.

We opened the door to the blast of noise and conversation and much excitement. Everybody was letting down after the tension of the two shows, and they were seated at big round tables, downing big plates of food and refreshments. I picked a table right near the front where I could see everyone coming in and going out, and eased myself into a chair. That's practically the first party I can remember where I didn't table-hop all evening. This time everybody table-hopped over to me. I stayed possibly half an hour or forty-five minutes, but in that time so many of the kids came over to say, "Thanks . . . I love being part of the show . . . I'm looking forward to the next one." And again and again, "Thanks. Thank you, Lawrence." The singers said it, the musicians said it, the stage crew said it and added how much they hoped we'd be back at ABC for our next season of taping. George sat down, beaming, hamburger in hand, and said, "Well, Lawrence, twenty-five years tonight! How about that? Twenty-five years together!" "George," I said, pained, "don't tell me I've put up with you for only twenty-five years! Seems more like fifty!" "Yeah, to me, too," said George cheerfully. Sam said much the same thing . . . only for him it was thirty years . . . and so did Don. I was surrounded by the physical evidence of many years of togetherness— friendships that went back a quarter of a century, roots that were interwined so deeply with mine we had become as one.

I wanted to stand up and make a speech to the folks. (I wanted to . . . but I couldn't!) I wanted to tell them that even though we had not yet received confirmation of our renewal for the next year, I felt absolutely confident that we would. I felt, with every fiber in my being, that the way they had worked, the sustained quality of the shows they had put together, the tremendous cooperation and goodwill they showed constantly—all of these would be rewarded with another season on TV. I'm not a betting man, but if I were, I would have bet on that.

But, of course, it was much too noisy for me to make speeches of any kind. So rather than put a damper on the party, I gathered my group together and we slipped out very quietly and drove home . . . and then I went back to bed with my heating pad!

But I couldn't get to sleep. At first I lay there in a warm and happy glow (partly from the heating pad, I suppose) . . . but mostly from the plain and simple gratitude and joy I felt for the kids whom I had just left at the party. For the twenty-fifth consecutive year my kids had brought us safely home again. We had stayed together, holding hands in a sense, climbing that mountain together. And we had made it. I was very, very happy.

*   *   *

But then, unhappily, I began to realize something. I began to realize that wonderful as our System was, and as powerful as it had just proved itself to be, I still couldn't recommend it to other businessm n! Not while there were so many restrictions and regulations to contend with. It just wasn't fair to them.

We had been able to operate successfully in spite of all the restrictions, true, but that was mainly because we had started back in the days when there weren't quite so many of them, and we had more or less learned to live with them over the years. But I just didn't feel I could ask other businessmen to accept our System of helping young people when I knew in advance what masses of red tape they'd have to face. It brought me down very badly. For the very first time, I began to realize what a lucky, lucky young man I was to have left the farm at the time I did.

19

MY AMERICA, YOUR AMERICA

WHEN I STARTED OUT in 1924, there were no rules prohibiting me from working till I reached a certain age, no laws which decreed what I had to be paid, no union mandates dictating to musicians. Instead, I found freedom . . . and a world where it was still possible to succeed if you put your whole heart and soul into it and worked with everything that was in you. I think now, that I was actually stepping into the last days of the free-enterprise system at a time when men were still able to compete with each other freely to produce the best possible product. I, myself, was surely proof of that! I certainly wasn't the best accordionist around, but I worked so hard on myself, learning other things about my profession, that I managed to make it anyway. It was really the help of George T. Kelly, who took me in on a free-enterprise basis, sharing profits with me, who gave me such a wonderful boost. Those were the days, and that was a time when conditions allowed us to live up to every bit of potential we had.

I don't think it was until about twelve years later that I began to run into restraints and restrictions so commonplace today. By then, fortunately, I'd been around long enough to have some stability. And I'd learned enough . . . and earned enough! . . . to tide me over. (I had moved to Omaha, Nebraska, from Yankton on the advice of a union friend of mine who told me the prospects in Omaha were much brighter. He was right, too. Omaha had a couple of big hotels and amusement centers where I could have played on a steady basis. The only trouble was, I couldn't get a union card. I never did find out why, but eventually I had to sell our home and take to the road again.) It seems to me now, looking back, that this type of thing tended to increase in size and scope from then on, taking over more and more of our lives and contributing greatly, in my opinion, to the downfall of the Big Bands. By now, I'm afraid we've gotten so far away from the essence and pure spirit of free enterprise we're in danger of losing it completely. And I'm very, very concerned. Free enterprise is inextricably bound up with freedom itself. And I have a strong, almost overpowering, conviction that if we lose one, we lose the other . . . and both are vital to our way of life.

Sometimes when I look at our young people today, my heart just aches for them. They just don't have the advantages I had. They don't have the freedom or the opportunity to try different jobs, to make mistakes, to grow, to work and find out what it takes to make it in this life.

Sometimes I let my mind wander, and I dream of an ideal situation, one in which we would all be free to try out our dreams. And I think . . . wouldn't it be nice if a businessman could find a youngster, perhaps a young boy, who seems right for his business or profession (whatever it is) and who could invite that boy to work with him for perhaps an hour or so, just so they'd get to know each other. And then—if there seems to be a mutual rapport—invite the boy to work for a full day or a week. By the end of that time, both of them would know pretty well whether they were suited to each other and would like to develop the relationship further. And then . . . in my dream . . . such a man would talk with the boy's parents or guardian and settle on a reasonable wage, something to maintain the young person while he's learning the fundamentals of his new craft. There would be no contracts, no legal restraints to tie the youngster up in bondage or commit the employer to any kind of permanent relationship. Everything would be free and open. Everything would hinge on how satisfying this mutual exchange of services and talents would be. The businessman would pass on his knowledge, his expertise, his personal guidance. The young person would bring his vitality, his freshness and eagerness to the business. Each would be taking the first few steps toward what could be a lifelong relationship, something which could add great happiness to the lives of both.

And then, in my ideal situation, the employer and trainee would continue to work together on this basis for a year, renegotiating the salary as the young person's skill increases. At the end of the year, if everyone agrees . . . and the apprenticeship having been served, so to speak . . . the youngster would graduate into the ranks of full-time employees. Again he and the employer would work out a fair salary and, in addition, the newcomer would then begin to share fully in the profits and other benefits of the company. He would, in effect, become a part owner of the organization, both in fact and in spirit. And he would have found his way in life.

All this could be done without any of the regulations and restrictions which now overwhelm and discourage so many businessmen. It could be done freely, voluntarily, and simply; without involving the government, the unions, or the schools; without getting enmeshed in work permits, contracts, or sanctions of various kinds; without the red tape which almost engulfs us these days. It could be done so simply . . . just two people committing themselves to try and bring out the best in each other.

But I suppose that's just a dream. It's not possible, in the light of what we have today in our national life.

But maybe not. Maybe it's not just a dream. Maybe the government, seeing the tremendous advantages of a private businessman taking on the responsibility of training and developing a young person at no cost to either the trainee or the government could make it possible. Maybe the government could give permission— a dispensation, so to speak—to any businessman willing to train young people and then share his business with them . . . and simply "excuse" him from existing rules and regulations. I'll go further than that—maybe the government could offer a tax break to such a businessman. A tax credit would be an extra incentive. (And also, human nature being what it is, a tax credit would tend to keep an employer on his very best behavior . . . he wouldn't want to lose it!) Actually, however, I feel our System is self-regulating, because any employer who failed to treat his employees the way they should be treated, would soon find that our System simply wouldn't work for him. None of his people would stay with him.

I just don't know how to go about getting this kind

of permission from the government . . . whether to press for some new kind of legislation (although my instincts are certainly against that! I think we're "overlawed" as it is).

But perhaps the government could study our musical organization as an already tested Pilot Program, and see the value inherent in our system of training and preparing young people for life—and take some positive action.

I hope this will happen. Because I feel with all my heart that our System could help to rescue our free-enterprise system from oblivion, and I yearn to do everything I can to save it. Free enterprise is what distinguishes us from other nations—the concept which has always said, "I'm an American, and I have the freedom and opportunity to follow my dreams." I want to ensure that our children will have that privilege, too. Free enterprise is the only way.

I would love to see an America in which all kinds of businesses were allowed to flourish—union, government, and profit-sharing businesses such as the one I've been describing. None of them need infringe on the other. All of them can work side by side, supplementing each other. In fact, a youngster trained in our System could most certainly join the union as a fully-qualified professional later on, if he so desired. And that would be fine, because each of us should be free to work in whatever system pleases and serves us best. Each of us should have the right of free choice.

Shall I tell you how I visualize an America in which our System would be allowed to function freely?

I see an America with hundreds of thousands of skilled and self-supporting young people—youngsters whose busy and happy lives would keep them from the deadly pleasures which lie in wait for those with nothing to occupy their minds or their time. I see young people whose strong and growing character would infuse our country with new strength, new growth. I see better products, a healthier moral climate, an increased demand for perfection in all walks of life. I see young folks being taught *how* to work and encouraged and guided into lives of personal achievement and responsibility, instead of being shielded from life, held back from competition and taught constantly, by direction and indirection, to expect others to do things for them. I see each one of us taking hold again of the ideals which inflamed the hearts of our grandparents and great-grandparents and realizing again—and forever—how tremendous are the principles of freedom which brought our country into being. I see us taking pride in our ability to take care of ourselves, but I also see us taking care of the weaker members in our midst with true compassion and love—those who are old and ill, mentally or physically handicapped, all those whose lives are too harsh, too difficult to bear alone. That is not only our duty, it is our privilege, something we should be proud and happy to do for those who need it.

But not for those of us who can take care of ourselves! Not for you and for me and the overwhelming majority of Americans who still believe in God and each other and the destiny of this country, those of us who are willing to stand alone and do it ourselves! It is my earnest wish and prayer that those of you who are reading my book and feel as I do, will think about it and join in this effort to give back to America the God-centered standards of honor and decency and personal responsibility; who cheerfully accept—in fact, insist—on the right to do things for ourselves, to face life on our own, not as weak people depending on others to take care of us, but as strong citizens living up to the potential God gave us . . . living up to the very best that is within us.

Then I see an America—my America, your America—living forever. In peace. In pride. And in freedom.

20

GOD'S LAWS

THE YEAR WAS OVER and I felt a kind of peace. I'm always grateful for my many blessings, but it seemed to me I'd had more than usual this year. We were still together—still had our health. My Musical Family was growing and constantly discovering new potential within itself. The Semonskis had made enough progress to justify the faith I'd had both in them and in our System. Bernice and I had worked hard on the book, but it had given me real joy to do so. I was filled with gratitude and contentment—never more than when I first rose in the morning. Always I was struck with the beauty that surrounded me . . . the hills beneath me, the ocean beyond . . . and so many times I would say to myself, "How beautiful this is! How lucky I am to be able to live here." And later, as I had breakfast with Fern, I'd look out the window at the flowers, trees, and green lawns . . . and then across the table at the wife who had shared so many good years with me, and I'd think again, "How fortunate I am. The Lord has been so very, very good to us." Morning prayers came very easily then— my heart was so full.

Nobody knows better than I how blessed I've been. I have practically everything a man could want in this world—a good wife, loving children, fine grandchildren, a career I love, fans whose affection has meant the world to me—and I am deeply grateful for all these wonderful blessings. But there is one thing for which I am most grateful of all, and that is my great fortune in having been born into a family which believed in God.

I couldn't survive without my faith. In fact, on those early morning swims of mine, I often reflect . . . I wouldn't even be here today to enjoy my blessings, if I hadn't learned long ago to follow the Laws of God.

Those teachings, ingrained into me from birth by my parents . . . and the good priests and patient nuns . . . became such a part of me, they provided me with the strength I needed when I needed it. That's not to say I have never fallen, never sinned. Of course I have. I'm as human as anyone else, and I think my passions are just as strong. But God's Laws have helped me to face up to my weaknesses and gain better control of myself.

My parents made God and the church the center of our lives. We never missed mass—never—no matter what the weather. Church on Sunday was as much a part of our lives as getting up in the morning, eating, sleeping. And the music in the church was a big part of our lives, too. I heard that glorious music from infancy, and it may have had more of an effect on me than I realized.

Yet I don't believe my brothers and sisters and I were really aware at the time that we were being taught God's Laws, the revealed truth of God, because my

parents lived the rules more than they talked about
them. It may be that I am seeing my parents through
a mist of love and years . . . and they may not have been
quite as saintly as I remember them. But I think it's
fair to say that both of them—my mother, in particular—lived their faith. And it had a powerful effect on
us children. My mother never preached much to us
boys . . . she just prayed a lot! . . . and we absorbed
the lessons by example.

In our community, marriage was for life and adultery
the worst sin of all, and I accepted that teaching so
completely that it was a terrible shock to me when I
went out into the world and discovered there were people who didn't always stick to their marriage vows! I
was so naive in those days it seems almost unbelievable.
There were times when I thought perhaps I had been
overprotected, growing up in such a simple, God-fear-
ing community. But today I know it was the greatest
blessing of my life. It gave me an unshakable belief in
God's Laws—an armor to meet life's battles.

As I grew older I could see the truth of those laws
for myself. I met people, good people, who were looking desperately for happiness—trying to find it through
drinking, drugs, sex. But they never found it that way.
They were perfect examples of something my very dear
friend Lon Varnell pointed out to me, years and years
later. "Nobody," he said, "can break God's Laws. The
only thing that breaks is the person who tries to do so."

I have tremendous gratitude in my heart that the
Good Lord saw fit to save me, because I know I would
have fallen time and time again without those solid,
undeviating principles. Nor could I have learned the
truly important things of life without that solid foundation. Where else could I have learned to feel the pure
gratitude I do for our audience—that wonderful, won-

derful audience who saved us—for the television stations, the arena managers, and all the other good friends who have helped us over the years? Where else could I have learned the gratitude and deep love I feel for my wonderful right-hand people who have stayed with me for so long, or the kids who have made my life such a joy, or learned to be honestly grateful for the setbacks and failures which in the long run serve only to purify us and make us stronger? God's immutable laws let you see things more clearly and keep your values straight.

I have tried, all through this book and all through my life, to convey the truths which I feel with all my heart lead to a better and happier life. I believe in them, just as I believe that the System we use in our Musical Family can help develop us into the strong and vital people we all want to be. But when you analyze all these guidelines, all these principles, and follow them back to their source, their roots, you will find they lead straight back to God's Laws. *They* are the real power of life.

I believe we need them more than ever today. It has always seemed reasonable to me that we became a strong nation in the first place because the people who came here believed in God, read their Bibles, and thanked the Good Lord for leading them to this country. They raised their families and built this nation according to God's Laws, and it was only when we moved away from this position that we became weakened and lost the source of our real strength.

As I said, I am absolutely convinced to the depths of my soul that I wouldn't be here at all today . . . wouldn't have the wonderfully satisfying life that has come to me through my family, my Musical Family, and our wonderful fans—had I not followed God's Laws. It has been hard to do occasionally, but I'm equally convinced God sends us adversity from time to time to make us stronger and better. The power and simplicity and effectiveness of those basic moral codes have been proven to me over and over and over again. I cannot think of one single problem in life—of those that arise in the relationship between men and women, or within a family or a business or a nation, which cannot be solved by going directly to the truths revealed to us through Divine Guidance.

If we treated each other with the kindness and honesty and justice God asks of us—how perfect life could be! I don't suppose we can ever reach that state of perfection, because we are all imperfect human beings with desires that often lead us astray, and emotions which tend to overwhelm us. But we are also human beings with the courage and free will to try constantly to do better. God's Laws can help us live a truly fulfilled life. Not necessarily a life filled only with pleasure, but a life that is fulfilled, in every sense of the word.

When I speak of God's Laws, I am not speaking of any particular church laws, but rather of all the Judeo-Christian ethics on which our country was founded— the Ten Commandments, the Sermon on the Mount, the Golden Rule. None of these is hard to find nor are they hard to understand. On the contrary, they are extremely simple and very explicit! They're hard to follow sometimes, that's true, but that's only because they recognize how frail and weak we human beings are, and they call on us to overcome our shortcomings and live up to the best that's in us.

I want so much for our young people—for all people—to understand that nothing worthwhile in life comes easily. The peace of mind and tremendous joy which come from following God's Laws are worth every sacrifice.

I have learned a good many lessons during my journey through life . . . some easy, some painful. And I have tried and will continue to try till the last days of my life to help others learn from those same truths. But if I had to choose just one . . . just one statement of faith, one message for the children of the world and the nation I love so much . . . it would still be the simple and powerful lesson I learned so many years ago at my mother's knee, as she sat in her little rocking chair in that small farmhouse in Strasburg: The greatest happiness in life comes from following God's Laws.

And if the world could only learn this . . . what a wonderful world it would be.

SOME "POST-SCRIPTS" FROM LAWRENCE

ONE AFTERNOON DURING THE writing of this book, Barney Liddell came bursting into my dressing room at the studio, waving some papers at me. "Lookit what I found, Boss!" he cried. "I was going through some old luggage in my attic yesterday and I found this—it must be the first band letter you ever wrote to us!"

I looked at the date, April 26, 1956. That meant I had written it just a few months after our national television debut on July 2, 1955 . . . certainly a high and very crucial point in our lives. I read it with great interest and noticed that two of the things I had stressed so strongly then, I am still stressing today . . . namely, pleasing our audience and striving constantly for perfection.

I still write these "band letters" at the beginning and end of every season—and in between times, too, if ever I feel there's a need for them! I've found I can accomplish more with these personal communications than with a generalized meeting, and I use them to motivate our people, set up goals for all of us, keep us close together as a family . . . and constantly aware of our obligations to our audience and each other.

I thought you might be interested in reading my first letter to the members of the band.

April 26, 1956

Dear Champagne Music Makers:

In our recent tours around the country, the most frequent comment I heard about us was that we are such a happy and contented group—that we look so happy on television—and that we sincerely enjoy playing for the public. And, more importantly that we genuinely *like* the people for whom we are playing.

If this is so, I think it is because of our one basic aim—"a desire to please"—not ourselves, but others. The desire to please is the KEYNOTE of our band and its success; it's been foremost in our minds throughout the twenty-seven years we've been building our band, and it is a *"natural"* policy, not one aimed at profit or success.

Pleasing those we play for should remain our first concern—as a group and as individuals—above anything else. To ignore this one great quality is to lose our audience—and it is surprising how fast an audience *can* be lost.

A grumpy face or attitude—magnified by the television screen in millions of homes throughout America —can overnight lose practically everything for which a group has been working. Obvious disharmony or lack of enthusiasm can easily bring the same result. This —despite the fact that a band might well be the greatest musical group in show business.

If you doubt it, fellows—look around you! Look at all the great bands we've all known, which were riding high on the waves of popularity, doing record business and then . . . almost overnight . . . passed right out of the show-business picture.

Why? How? Either because they had disharmony among themselves, which was reflected in their performance, or because they had so fallen in love with the pleasures of playing music for themselves . . . rather than for the enjoyment of the public . . . that their public soon tired of admiring a group which obviously admired itself sufficiently. Of course, there may have been other contributing factors in their downfall, but believe me, *these* were probably the *major points* involved!

How do we Champagne Music Makers fit into this picture? Maybe some of us fail to see the significance of these statements and facts. But this isn't just something of vague interest to us. It's *vital* to us and our continued welfare.

We're riding pretty high now. Our ratings are coming along fine. We are seen every Saturday evening by some thirty million people—many of them ardent Champagne Music Fans. We all receive letters by the mail-sack full, every week. We have a "permanent" home at the Aragon Ballroom, which allows us to stay in Ocean Park and Los Angeles and live like ordinary people. Our family life is something that few musical groups have. We can enjoy being with our wives, our children, and our own group of friends. We all enjoy fine incomes, which are the envy of every other orchestra in show business. We are in the most enviable position of any band in the country.

Should we start to forget these benefits—these wonders we have all worked so hard for and have finally achieved—we're likely to find ourselves in the same spot in which too many other bands have found themselves—with our solid foundation washed away from under us, looking around for solid ground to walk on again.

Fellows, we have three major responsibilities to ourselves as individuals . . . and to all of us as a group: (1) *to continue to be good musicians;* (2) to continue working together in complete harmony, thereby reflecting a likable personality; and (3) to continue in our dèsire to please our audiences and our working partners.

If we can continue to achieve these three objectives, our Success Story can continue for a long time to come, and—more importantly—we can continue to live with ourselves.

The most important word in the language of Man is the word YOU. Talk to someone about himself, and he'll listen for hours. Talk to him in a newspaper or magazine advertisement about what *your* product can do for HIM, and he'll devour every word you've written. On the other hand, if you tell him all about *yourself,* and what a wonderful fellow YOU are, he'll soon find something else to occupy his attention.

Just as true is the fact that, to us Champagne Music Makers, the most important people in our world are our AUDIENCES—the people who tune us in, who flock to the Aragon to dance to our music. If we were to play merely for our own amusement, we all know we'd soon be without fans. They'd find another band to admire. It is to *them* we must devote our time and our thoughts and our efforts, because their like or dislike of us can make us highly successful—or "hasbeens."

An entertainer who doesn't care about people cannot truly entertain them, because he's too interested in his own feelings to care about theirs—and they can sense this.

"Perfection is the One Thing in the World which can never be achieved," is an old saying. But Perfection is the one thing we must strive for constantly. Because the closer we can get to Perfection . . . the happier we will be—each of us, and all of us.

YOUR personal success is perhaps the most important thing in MY life—except for my family. This is true, simply because of the fact that if YOU are a success, if YOU are happy, we all will be.

Discontent or disharmony can do irreparable harm, so if you ever do have anything troubling you, I hope you'll let me work with you toward a happy solution—for the betterment of yourself, and the betterment of all of us.

Best personal regards and good wishes to you and to your families.

Yours cordially,

Musical Family Golden Rules

So MANY TIMES—ESPECIALLY when we're out on tour
—people ask me what kind of rules and regulations we
use to keep our kids behaving so well! Actually, we
don't have any specific rules and regulations. But, as I
worked on this book, I began to realize we do have our
"unwritten" rules, our own basic beliefs, which have
come about almost automatically because of the close
and warm way we work together. First and foremost
among these is the recognition that we're all here for one
purpose in life—to love and serve God and develop
the potentials and talents He gave us to the very best
of our ability. And secondly . . . that we're privileged to
work together in freedom, with equal justice for all, and
special privilege for none. With these two principles as
our basic foundation, we have developed our own set
of precepts and guidelines, our own Musical Family
Golden Rules, and here they are:

1. Punctuality   If everyone is not on time for

rehearsal . . . and we condone it just once . . . we're already in a certain amount of trouble!

2. Preparation

Preparation is my number one requirement. I can't stress it strongly enough. Without preparation, the show would really be in trouble!

3. Discipline and Obedience

I recognize that this concept has lost much of its attraction today, but I believe it is vital to a smooth-running show.

4. Honesty and Truthfulness

With these two great qualities, an organization has real security.

5. Cleanliness and Wholesomeness, Inside and Out

Not only on the show but everywhere . . . at home and away from home.

6. Humility

There is great need for this, especially in our business. Applause doesn't help!

7. Work!

Work is not a dirty word. Find the work you love and it will become a joy.

8. Do It Yourself

The best way to learn.

9. Give Freely of Yourself

This invariably brings great joy and fulfillment.

10. No Contracts

This builds a powerful trust between both parties and permits them to develop their highest potential in complete freedom.

Writing down these Golden Rules for our Musical Family made me feel it wouldn't hurt if we had a similar list for our great American family! I believe with all my heart that if we are to survive as the greatest civilized democratic society in the history of the world, then we must retain and strengthen certain basic precepts that are part of our American heritage. Among these are:

Freedom

Freedom is, without doubt, the greatest blessing we have in America. Let us protect and defend it with all our hearts, all our energies.

Free Enterprise

Free enterprise goes hand in hand with freedom. Protecting our individual right to free enterprise is basic to our way of life.

High Moral Standards

We need to remember that money is not success, and permissiveness does not breed happiness. Money—or rather, the love of money—can cause more heartbreak and disaster than almost anything else. And losing your life in permis-

194

siveness means losing every chance for lasting happiness.

Financial
Responsibility

I'm famous for being thrifty, I guess! But I do feel our nation could benefit from controlling our spending. One way to do this would be to try out new ideas on a small scale in one state or locality, before putting them into effect nationwide. I think if "bussing," for example, or "seat-belts," or any number of other ideas had been put to a pilot-program test beforehand, it could have saved us numerous headaches and heartaches—as well as money.

Opportunity

Let's keep the door of opportunity open for everyone, especially for our young people, and enact whatever legislation is necessary to give them the training, the help, the encouragement they need to become self-supporting, self-confident, and self-sufficient adults.

Compassion

Let us never forget to help those among us who need it. But let us also never forget to develop those who are able, into the strong and dedicated kind of citizens our country must have.

Religious Beliefs

This country was founded on our belief in God. We wrote it into our Constitution, carved it on our federal buildings, engraved it on our money.

Let us never forget that God gave us life, and a chance to live it to His glory—and our own fulfillment. The best way we can do that, for ourselves and others, is through the medium of work—service—and love.

Short Outline of the Lawrence Welk Musical Family Training and Sharing Plan

THE WELK TRAINING AND Sharing Plan is an adaptation of the free-enterprise system, in which an employer and employee voluntarily agree to exchange mutual services. The employer agrees to train and develop a potential employee through actual on-the-job work experience; the employee agrees to give his fullest cooperation and best talents. The hoped-for-goal for both is full employment for the employee, plus a share in the profits of the organization.

It is understood by both parties that neither is under obligation to the other. Everything is on a free and voluntary basis. There are no contracts involved.

The Plan is divided into three basic parts:

I

Training Program

1. All training is done on the job, by the employer and senior employees.
2. Trainees are paid a wage during training period.
3. Training period is not to exceed one year.
4. At the end of the year, employer and employee review progress and decide whether to continue their relationship. If the trainee becomes a full employee, he begins, from that day on, to share in the profits and other benefits of the business.

II

Sharing Program

1. Employer shares profits with employees at the end of every year. In our Teleklew Corporation, we set aside an amount of money equal to fifteen percent of our annual gross payroll, the maximum amount allowed by law. This money is deposited into a special fund maintained and invested for the sole benefit of the employees.

2. The entire profit-sharing program is funded completely by management.

3. Employees receive their share of this fund when they retire or leave the organization.

4. The employer also shares other benefits, in order to reward and stimulate above-average performance. Whenever someone does an outstanding job, the employer recognizes it with a special award. This could be anything from a bonus check to a personalized gift, always something designed particularly for that person's needs or wishes. This helps motivate continued excellence of performance, and builds a strong personal relationship.

5. Teleklew also assumes all or part of the payment for medical coverage, life insurance, union assessments, etc.

SOME "POSTSCRIPTS" FROM LAWRENCE

We make a continual study of the conditions and factors that can be most helpful and beneficial to our employees, and because of this kind of thinking we have developed the most important "sharing" of all, the intangible spiritual sharing which results in a warm and close family feeling. This is invaluable, not only for the joy in work it brings, but also because it invariably results in producing a superior product, which is, or should be, a major goal in any business enterprise.

III

No Contracts

We have no contracts with our people. Everything is on a free and voluntary basis. We all realize that the only way to maintain our record of achievement is to *continuously* do the best possible job for each other. The "No Contracts" policy stimulates top-quality performance, plus a mutual regard for, and trust in each other.

THE PRIME GOAL OF OUR JOB TRAINING AND SHARING PROGRAM IS TO DEVELOP THE INDIVIDUAL PERSON TO THE HIGHEST POSSIBLE DEGREE OF HIS INBORN TALENTS AND POTENTIAL IN EVERY WAY—PERSONALLY, PROFESSIONALLY, MORALLY, AND SPIRITUALLY. THIS GOAL IS THE BASIC, UNDERLYING MOTIVATION FOR OUR ENTIRE SYSTEM.

I THOUGHT PERHAPS YOU might also like to see this note from Meredith Willson, with its charming little signature, because it expresses so beautifully how I feel about gratitude. Meredith never fails to send us a personal, hand-written note whenever we play one of his wonderful songs . . . in this case, it was "Seventy-Six Trombones" . . . and his notes give me such great pleasure I sometimes think I'd play one of his songs for the sheer joy of getting one of his notes! Of course we don't do that, we play the Music Man's beautiful melodies simply because they're such great favorites with the American audience. But receiving such a lovely, thoughtful letter makes our pleasure just twice as great. Gratitude is like that. It blesses whomever and whatever it touches.

March 8 '76

Dear Lawrence —

Rosemary and I are still re-living our delightful evening with you and your fabulous Broadcast-Telecast. Our phone hasn't stopped ringing — from "Everybody-and-his-brother"!

Man! do you have an audience!! We heard from people we scarcely know — and from folks we hadn't heard from since High School Days! And their grown-up young-ones — and their young-ones! (Do you have a sharp bunch of fans!) Our thanks, dear Lawrence; our admiration; and our love.

Meredith

— may the good Lord bless/keep you —

203

March 3, 1976

Dear Mr. Welk,

Now that the taping of our first season is completed, we just wanted to tell you how much we loved working with you and your wonderful group. Everyone is so kind and friendly and each one as talented as the other.

We especially appreciate the help of Gail Farrell and the patience of George Cates and Bob Ballard. They helped us greatly to improve our singing.

But, of course, you are the only reason we are here. You gave us the opportunity to sing on your show, work with these people, and to make something of our lives. We love singing together so much, and we hope to make a lot of people happy. Thanks to you we can. There aren't too many people in your position who would hire a family as big as ours and care for them the way you cared for us. You've become like our own grandfather.

We will always be grateful to you, but the only way we can repay you is through our singing. You have given so much of yourself and that is the only thing you have asked of us.

We promise not to let you down.

Love from all,

The Semonski Family

I WAS VERY HAPPY to receive this letter. It conveys what I've been trying to point out in this book. Look at the closing line. I think it proves that if you give young folks a helping hand and let them know you believe in them, they are not going to let you down.

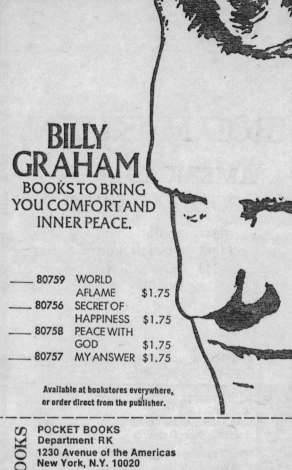
176